The History of the Police

CRAFTED BY SKRIUWER

Copyright © 2025 by Skriuwer.

All rights reserved. No part of this book may be used or reproduced in any form whatsoever without written permission except in the case of brief quotations in critical articles or reviews.

At **Skriuwer**, we're more than just a team—we're a global community of people who love books. In Frisian, "Skriuwer" means "writer," and that's at the heart of what we do: creating and sharing books with readers worldwide. Wherever you are in the world, **Skriuwer** is here to inspire learning.

Frisian is one of the oldest languages in Europe, closely related to English and Dutch, and is spoken by about **500,000 people** in the province of **Friesland** (Fryslân), located in the northern Netherlands. It's the second official language of the Netherlands, but like many minority languages, Frisian faces the challenge of survival in a modern, globalized world.

We're using the money we earn to promote the Frisian language.

For more information, contact : **kontakt@skriuwer.com** (www.skriuwer.com)

Disclaimer:
The images in this book are creative reinterpretations of historical scenes. While every effort was made to accurately capture the essence of the periods depicted, some illustrations may include artistic embellishments or approximations. They are intended to evoke the atmosphere and spirit of the times rather than serve as precise historical records.

TABLE OF CONTENTS

CHAPTER 1

- Emergence of basic guardians and local enforcers in early communities
- Role of temple guards, religious authority, and rudimentary administrative systems
- Influence of ancient Mesopotamia, Egypt, and other early civilizations on law enforcement

CHAPTER 2

- Formation of city-states in regions like Sumer, Phoenicia, and early Greece
- Transition from volunteer watch systems to more formal guard units
- Development of local laws, councils, and magistrates for maintaining public order

CHAPTER 3

- The Vigiles, Praetorian Guard, and Urban Cohorts as Roman security pillars
- Blend of firefighting, night patrol, and imperial protection
- Long-term influence on European administrative structures post-Rome

CHAPTER 4

- Feudal watch and ward, castle-based security, and local authority of lords
- Sheriff, reeve, and tithing responsibilities in rural communities
- Role of the Church in moral policing and dispute resolution

CHAPTER 5

- Evolution of the English sheriff (shire-reeve) and constable offices
- Collaboration between local assemblies, parishes, and royal authority
- Influence on later British colonies and broader common-law policing models

CHAPTER 6

- Muhtasib and qadi roles in the Islamic world's market and moral enforcement
- Chinese yamen magistrates, constables, and the baojia collective responsibility system
- Ottoman and Persian structures blending religious authority with state administration

---

CHAPTER 7

- Centralizing tendencies under absolute monarchies, growing bureaucracies
- City guards, watchmen, and specialized officials during the Renaissance/Reformation
- Rise of standing forces for maintaining urban security and preventing revolts

---

CHAPTER 8

- Transplant of sheriff-constable systems to the Americas, Africa, and Asia
- Paramilitary forces enforcing colonial rule and economic interests
- Blend of indigenous customs with European frameworks, often creating hybrid structures

---

CHAPTER 9

- Secret police networks, royal edicts, and militarized gendarmeries
- Role of cardinals, advisers, and ministerial offices in France, Russia, and other states
- Emergence of centralized law enforcement as a tool for sustaining autocratic power

---

CHAPTER 10

- Philosophical critiques of arbitrary rule and harsh punishments
- Cesare Beccaria's influence on proportionality and rational law enforcement
- Foundational ideas for humane treatment and emphasis on public accountability

CHAPTER 11

- Ministry of General Police in France and the Prefecture of Police in Paris
- Exportation of Napoleonic administrative models across Europe
- Gendarmerie systems in rural areas, cementing centralized authority

CHAPTER 12

- Aftermath of Napoleonic wars, conservative restorations, and early liberal movements
- Growing municipal forces in Europe and North America in response to urbanization
- Debates over political dissent, secret police, and labor unrest shaping policing

CHAPTER 13

- Diverse indigenous methods of law enforcement, from tribal elders to religious courts
- Impact of Islam, Confucianism, and other cultural factors on policing
- Influence of early colonial contacts and eventual penetration by European frameworks

CHAPTER 14

- Colonial transplant of English constables, sheriffs, and night watches
- Distinct Southern slave patrols, linking policing to racial control
- Emergence of urban forces responding to industrial growth, immigration, and civic needs

CHAPTER 15

- Rapid urban expansion, labor conflicts, and new crime patterns
- Spread of professional, salaried forces to manage strikes, slums, and public disorder
- Growing adoption of centralized record-keeping and early detective techniques

CHAPTER 16

- Institutional consolidation of British and European police forces
- Focus on moral campaigns, detective work, and standardized training
- Public acceptance versus criticism of heavy-handed tactics and class bias

---

CHAPTER 17

- Global spread of uniformed, hierarchical police as a modern state hallmark
- Further professionalization through training schools, rank structures, and special units
- Persistent accountability issues, labor strikes, and class/racial inequalities

---

CHAPTER 18

- Rise of progressive politics, socialist agitation, and demands for civil liberties
- Improved investigative methods (fingerprinting, better forensics), early cross-border coordination
- Balance between service-oriented policing and political repression in a rapidly changing world

---

CHAPTER 19

- Nation-building efforts in newly unified or reorganized states
- Colonial policing at its peak, with paramilitary control and forced labor systems
- Deepening scientific thought in criminology, sociopolitical reforms, and early moves toward transnational cooperation

---

CHAPTER 20

- Synopsis of historical progression from ancient watchmen to consolidated 19th-century forces
- Recurring tensions: corruption vs. professionalism, liberty vs. security, moral enforcement vs. personal freedoms
- Legacy for modern policing: hierarchical structures, investigative bureaus, community service ideals, and lingering social controversies

Chapter 1

Introduction: Policing in the Ancient World

Human history is filled with stories of people seeking order and security in their communities. From the very beginning of civilization, humans have needed ways to protect property, safeguard lives, and resolve disputes. These methods of maintaining peace and safety evolved into what we recognize today as policing. Yet policing, as a formal institution, did not appear out of thin air. In this chapter, we will explore how ancient societies first approached the challenge of order-keeping and why they felt it was necessary. We will look at the earliest known forms of police-like duties in communities, from small hunter-gatherer groups to the large empires of Mesopotamia and Egypt, and we will learn how these ancient forms of law enforcement set the stage for later developments.

The Roots of Social Order in Small Communities

Before large cities and organized states existed, humans lived in smaller groups. These groups might have been extended families, clans, or tribes. In these communities, social order often depended on customs and traditions passed down through generations. There were no formal laws written on tablets or in books, but there were commonly understood rules. These rules told people how to treat each other, how to share resources, and how to respect boundaries.

When disputes arose—maybe someone stole an animal or a piece of valuable goods—elders or respected figures in the group would step in to mediate. They might have no uniform or official title, but their authority was recognized because of their experience or wisdom. Sometimes these individuals were the strongest or most influential hunters or warriors. In other cases, they might be chosen because they were seen as fair and unbiased. While this setup might not look like policing as we know it, it fulfilled the same function: maintaining order and settling conflicts.

Punishments in these early societies varied. They could include banishment, fines in the form of goods, or in extreme cases, violence against the offender. The purpose was to maintain harmony within the group, because survival often required cooperation. If someone disrupted that cooperation, it threatened the entire group. Thus, the earliest "police work" was carried out by individuals who held the group's trust or fear, ensuring everyone followed common rules.

Emergence of Settlements and the Need for Organized Control

Over time, humans shifted from nomadic lifestyles to more settled ways of living. The development of agriculture allowed people to stay in one place and produce food. As farming became more advanced, communities grew larger. With larger communities came new problems—conflicts over land, water, food storage, and labor. There was now a need for a more structured way to maintain peace.

In these early settlements, people realized that casual, ad-hoc forms of dispute resolution were no longer enough. When a community had hundreds of people, not everyone was personally known or trusted by everyone else. This change prompted the creation of roles or committees within the community that focused on maintaining order. This might include:

1. **Community Watch:** A small group of individuals, often volunteers, who would walk around the settlement, especially at night, to watch out for thieves or fires.
2. **Designated Elders or Leaders:** Men and women selected by the group based on status, wealth, or wisdom to help settle more serious conflicts and lead discussions about common issues.
3. **Informal Agreements with Neighboring Settlements:** As communities expanded, they might forge pacts or treaties with nearby groups, agreeing not to raid or steal from each other, thus setting a precursor to inter-community policing.

Mesopotamia: The Cradle of Early Law and Enforcement

Mesopotamia is often referred to as the "cradle of civilization." It was located in what is now modern-day Iraq, encompassing the fertile region between the Tigris and Euphrates rivers. With its fertile land, it became home to some of the earliest cities, such as Uruk, Ur, and Babylon. Along with urban growth came the earliest known written law codes, the most famous being the **Code of Hammurabi** (circa 18th century BCE).

The Code of Hammurabi featured a wide range of laws about property, trade, family matters, and personal conduct. It also laid out punishments for breaking these laws. Because these laws existed in written form, there needed to be a group of officials responsible for enforcing them. Although ancient records do not always use the word "police," the people who enforced these rules performed functions similar to police work:

- **Execution of Law:** Officials or local leaders made arrests or summoned accused individuals to court.
- **Guarding Public Spaces:** Certain persons might watch over the markets, temples, or city gates to prevent theft or misconduct.
- **Tax Collection and Public Order:** Tax collectors, while mainly responsible for gathering revenues, often doubled as enforcers when someone did not pay or disrupted the tax process.

These early roles show that law enforcement was already being specialized to an extent. The combination of official authority, written law, and punishments enforced by recognized individuals is a hallmark of early policing in Mesopotamia.

Ancient Egypt: Guardians of the Pharaoh's Order

Ancient Egypt also had well-defined structures that served police-like functions. Egyptian society was highly stratified, with the Pharaoh at the top claiming divine authority. Below him were nobles, priests, scribes, and government officials. The administration was quite advanced for the time, making it possible to organize large-scale projects like pyramid construction or canal digging.

In Egyptian records, we see references to officials who might be called **"medjay"** during some periods, originally a name for people from a certain region who were recruited as guards or scouts. Over time, the term came to be used for a sort of paramilitary or policing force. Their tasks included:

1. **Protecting Trade Routes:** Egypt's wealth depended partly on trade, especially along the Nile. The medjay or other guard-like forces kept an eye out for bandits.
2. **Guarding Royal Tombs and Structures:** Tomb looting was a constant concern, so watchers and guards were placed around these sites.
3. **Dealing with Criminal Activity:** In large temple complexes or cities, these guards would settle minor disputes, detain suspected thieves, and bring them before local magistrates.

Beyond the medjay, there were also local officials responsible for collecting taxes, managing grain storage, and ensuring that peasants did not escape their labor obligations. While these roles were not labeled "police" in the modern sense, they served as important elements of social control. The Pharaoh's government had a vested interest in preventing anything that might undermine its power or damage the system of resource distribution.

Policing Duties Tied to Religious Authority

In many ancient cultures, religious institutions also played a key role in social control. Priests and temple staff were often involved in the community's legal affairs, partly because temples served as places of safety, record-keeping, and economic exchange. Since laws in many of these societies were thought to be derived from the gods, it made sense for religious figures to have some control in enforcing moral or legal norms.

For example, in ancient Mesopotamia, temple complexes had significant economic power, and temple staff could be part of local justice systems. Similarly, in Egypt, priests held high status and often had a say in resolving conflicts, especially if a matter was deemed to have a religious dimension. This kind of arrangement continued in various forms across different regions: religious institutions were natural partners in the maintenance of order because they influenced both moral guidelines and daily practices.

The Importance of Order for Public Works

A key aspect of these early civilizations was their focus on public works—building roads, temples, walls, irrigation systems, and so on. Maintaining a stable workforce for such projects required some form of policing. If large groups of laborers were forced or paid to work on these tasks, a certain level of supervision was needed to prevent rebellion, theft, or desertion. Officials in charge of these projects sometimes had specialized guards to keep watch over laborers, ensuring everyone stayed in line. These guards also handled disputes or fights that broke out among workers.

At the same time, a city or kingdom was always at risk of internal unrest. When people felt overtaxed, underfed, or mistreated by government officials, they might resist the authorities. Leaders learned quickly that if they wanted to keep control, they needed a reliable way to catch rebels or criminals before they stirred public anger. Hence, policing developed not just to protect people, but also to protect the interests of rulers and the upper classes who depended on social stability to remain in power.

Record-Keeping and the Growth of Bureaucracy

One of the big shifts from prehistoric to ancient times was the rise of writing and record-keeping. Policing benefited from this development. Officials could now keep track of crimes, taxes, and rulings in a more permanent form. In places like Mesopotamia, scribes played a vital role in documenting who owed fines or who had been accused of wrongdoing. This documentation provided a layer of consistency—no longer were disputes settled only on the memory of a local elder or chief. Instead, there were written records that could be referenced, and these often increased the power of those who controlled the records.

In ancient Egypt, scribes recorded not just the pharaoh's decrees but also local matters such as the distribution of grain. If someone stole grain from the communal store, that theft was noted, and punishments could be carried out methodically. This power of documentation meant that law enforcement officials, or those fulfilling that role, were backed by a system that could store and retrieve facts about people's behavior and obligations.

Early Concepts of Investigation and Punishment

While we don't have extensive details about the day-to-day investigative methods of ancient law enforcers, some clues do exist. For instance, when a theft occurred, local officials might question witnesses or check records. Sometimes they might rely on a form of primitive forensics, looking for footprints or forced entry. Punishments, as recorded in texts like the Code of Hammurabi, were often harsh—ranging from fines to corporal punishment or even the death penalty. The severity of these punishments was meant to deter future wrongdoing.

Even so, we can see that ancient law was not random. There were procedures, even if they varied from place to place. People accused of serious crimes might appear before a council or official for judgment. In some societies, there were also "divine tests," where the accused might have to undergo a challenge (such as stepping into dangerous water or handling a hot metal object) to prove innocence. Although this method was based on superstition, it reflected a structured approach to handling conflicts. Some official, in effect, oversaw these trials, providing a proto-police or judicial function.

Military and Policing Overlaps

In many ancient societies, the line between military service and policing duties was blurred. Armies were used not only for warfare but also for keeping the peace internally. Soldiers might be tasked with arresting rebels or suppressing local revolts. City walls, guard towers, and armed soldiers patrolling the perimeter served to protect against external threats but also stood as a visible reminder of the ruler's power over citizens.

An example of this overlap can be seen in empires like Assyria, where the king maintained a strong, well-organized army. That army was often stationed in conquered territories to prevent uprisings. Local populations quickly learned that the presence of these soldiers was as much about policing them as defending them from outside invasions. Over time, certain units might have specialized in controlling internal conflicts, performing duties that resemble police work more than battlefield combat.

Social Hierarchy and Law Enforcement

It is crucial to remember that in ancient times, society was not egalitarian. In most civilizations, strict hierarchies existed, and those at the bottom had fewer rights and protections. Slaves, servants, and lower-class workers often received the harshest treatments from law enforcers. Laws themselves reflected the social biases of the period. For example, under the Code of Hammurabi, punishments varied depending on whether the victim was a noble or a commoner. The same crime could receive drastically different sentences.

This reality meant that law enforcement in ancient times was not always about ensuring justice in the modern sense. It was equally about keeping the social order established by the ruling class or monarchy. Whether it was a city-state governed by a priest-king or an empire led by a pharaoh, the enforcement of laws usually served the powerful first.

Communication and the Spread of Policing Ideas

In ancient times, travel was slower and more dangerous than today, but trade routes still connected diverse cultures. People from different regions communicated ideas about governance, religion, and military tactics. Along with these ideas, methods of crime control and dispute resolution also spread. If one empire had success with a particular approach—such as using specialized guards for the marketplace—another might adopt or adapt that method. This is how certain policing principles, like patrolling or investigating, likely moved from one civilization to another.

For instance, the influence of Mesopotamian or Egyptian administrative practices can be seen in neighboring regions like the Levant, Anatolia (modern Turkey), and across the Mediterranean. Elements of these early systems became building blocks for later civilizations, including ancient Greece and Rome.

Summary of Key Points for Ancient World Policing

1. **Small Beginnings:** Early policing grew out of a need for order within small communities, usually led by elders or strong individuals.

2. **Rise of Cities and Laws:** As settlements became bigger, written laws emerged. People who enforced these laws acted as the first police-like officials.
3. **Religious and Government Roles:** Temples, priests, and scribes often handled legal matters, blending religious authority with social control.
4. **Military Overlap:** Armies and guards frequently performed policing duties, especially in large empires.
5. **Record-Keeping:** Written records and laws allowed for more consistent enforcement and a stronger bureaucracy.
6. **Social Hierarchy:** Enforcement typically benefited the ruling classes, and punishments varied by social status.
7. **Communication of Ideas:** Even in ancient times, methods of managing crime and disorder spread through trade and contact between different peoples.

These foundational elements of policing in the ancient world will frame our understanding of how policing became more organized over time. By looking at these early practices, we can see that the basic ideas of patrol, investigation, and social control were already forming thousands of years ago. Although these methods might seem primitive compared to what we have now, they were essential in shaping the path toward more complex and specialized law enforcement structures in later eras.

In the next chapter, we will move beyond these early beginnings to examine the growth of organized policing in the city-states that emerged around the world. These transitions from loosely defined roles to more formal ones set the stage for the classical civilizations and medieval societies that followed.

Chapter 2

Early City-States and the Growth of Organized Policing

In Chapter 1, we explored how policing duties took shape in the ancient world, focusing on basic forms of social control and the emergence of official enforcers tied to rulers or religious centers. In this chapter, we will dive deeper into the evolution of early city-states—politically independent urban centers that governed themselves and the surrounding territories—and how these developments led to more structured approaches to law enforcement. These new political entities required more reliable systems of maintaining order, collecting taxes, and overseeing public spaces, all of which contributed to the birth of more recognizable policing institutions.

Defining the City-State

A city-state is typically defined as a self-governing urban center that exercises authority over nearby lands, which might include smaller villages or farming areas. Unlike large empires that spanned wide territories, a city-state had a narrower geographic reach but a tightly knit political system. Some of the most famous examples of city-states include those in ancient Mesopotamia (like Ur and Uruk), in the Levant (such as the Phoenician city-states of Tyre and Sidon), and later in ancient Greece (Athens, Sparta, Corinth, and others).

City-states often faced unique challenges that set them apart from smaller communities:

1. **Population Density:** More people living in one place meant more potential for crime, disputes, and social unrest.
2. **Economic Activity:** Trade, craft production, and marketplaces thrived, but these activities also attracted thieves and fraud.
3. **Political Autonomy:** City-states had their own laws, government officials, and sometimes militaries, which included roles akin to police forces or guards.

Because of these factors, city-states were more likely to develop specialized roles for policing than loosely organized rural villages. Larger populations and active commerce put pressure on local leaders to find effective ways to preserve order.

Formal Laws and Specialized Roles

In city-states, the shift from unwritten customs to formal, codified laws became more pronounced. We see this in ancient Mesopotamian city-states that expanded on law codes like Hammurabi's. Likewise, city-states in ancient Greece developed laws that were etched into public spaces, so citizens could read and understand them. For instance, the laws of Athens were inscribed on wooden tablets or stone pillars known as axones and kyrbeis, placed in public view.

With written laws came the need for officials who were aware of these laws, could interpret them, and had the authority to enforce them. In some city-states, these officials were part of the ruling council, while in others, they belonged to a separate administrative body. Over time, a hierarchy formed:

1. **Lawmakers or Councils:** This group created or revised the laws.
2. **Judges or Magistrates:** They interpreted the laws in legal disputes, decided punishments, and sometimes supervised law enforcers.
3. **Guards or Watchmen:** They patrolled public areas, protected city gates, and apprehended suspects.
4. **Scribes or Clerks:** They recorded cases, kept track of punishments, and documented civil matters like contracts and wills.

While this breakdown might not have been as strictly defined in all city-states, it shows the natural progression toward specialized roles for policing and law enforcement.

Public Order in the Streets: Markets and Gatherings

One of the primary concerns for city-states was controlling public gatherings. Markets, festivals, and religious ceremonies brought large crowds into the city center. With so many people packed together, theft, fights, or riots could erupt. City-state leaders recognized the value of having designated individuals—guards or watchmen—who could keep an eye on these events and intervene if necessary.

For example, in ancient Greek city-states, **agoránomoi** were officials responsible for overseeing the marketplace (the **agora**). Their duties included regulating weights and measures, ensuring vendors complied with trade laws, and sometimes settling minor disputes on the spot. While they were not police in the strict modern sense, their role shared many similarities with policing: they enforced rules, handled complaints, and worked to prevent disorder in a public space.

Policing and City Walls

City-states often had walls and gates. These defensive structures protected inhabitants from outside attacks. Yet they also served another policing function: controlling who entered and left the city. Guards posted at gates would inspect travelers, collect tolls or taxes on goods, and watch for criminals or suspicious characters. Inside the city, watchtowers or guard posts might be located along the walls, allowing a small force of sentinels to survey the streets below.

In many city-states, the city walls were a symbol of civic pride. They demonstrated a sense of organization and unity, as building such extensive defenses required the efforts of many people. Guards were typically paid or given certain privileges by the city's government, marking the early stages of professional law enforcement. Rather than being volunteers or ad-hoc enforcers, these guards had assigned shifts, responsibilities, and standards of conduct (although these standards varied and were not as formally codified as modern policing codes).

The Role of Military Garrisons

In some city-states, maintaining a small standing army or local militia was key to security. These forces were usually trained for warfare but had peacetime duties that overlapped with policing. Soldiers could be deployed to quell uprisings, enforce curfews, or protect important officials. When a city-state conquered another, it might station troops in the conquered city to ensure compliance with new laws and tribute requirements.

Because these soldiers were often the only organized, armed group in the city-state, they naturally took on tasks that involved forceful control of the population. This arrangement could be beneficial for rulers, but it also risked abuses of power. Without checks and balances, a military force acting as police could engage in extortion or violence against citizens. Nevertheless, this overlap of military and police roles was common in ancient times and would continue in various forms throughout history.

Investigating Crimes and Resolving Disputes

While the concept of investigation was still limited by the era's technology and understanding of evidence, city-states made efforts to look into crimes more systematically than smaller villages. A murder or theft in a city-state often involved official inquiries. Witnesses might be called, and testimony was taken. Sometimes, city leaders employed **public criers** who would announce crimes or lost property, asking for information or assistance from citizens.

In many Greek city-states, the practice of seeking justice was partly communal: citizens had a civic duty to report crimes and sometimes to apprehend criminals if they were caught in the act. The state encouraged citizens to be active in maintaining order, because the well-being of the entire city was at stake. If a city-state had a strong cultural identity, citizens might feel a sense of pride in defending the laws, which were often seen as integral to their way of life.

Punishments in city-states could be severe, especially for crimes that threatened the community's stability. Exile was a common penalty for serious offenses, effectively banishing the individual from the city. For repeated or especially harmful crimes, the death penalty might be used. Lesser crimes could result in fines, compensation to the victim, or forced labor. The threat of these punishments helped leaders maintain order, but they also had to ensure procedures were somewhat fair, otherwise unrest could grow.

Religious Festivals, Civic Pride, and Crowd Control

Religion and civic pride were deeply intertwined in city-states. Large festivals honoring gods or celebrating military victories could attract thousands of people. For a few days, normal business might stop, and the city would be filled with feasts, processions, music, and dancing. While these events provided unity and excitement, they also posed significant risks: crowd crush, drunken brawls, or opportunistic criminals. As a result, specialized teams were sometimes assigned to manage the flow of people, keep an eye on suspicious activity, and respond to emergencies.

Some city-states even developed rudimentary crowd-control tactics. They might set designated paths for processions or place city guards at strategic points to funnel people in certain directions. If problems occurred, guards would attempt to break up fights or pull aside troublemakers, bringing them to a local magistrate for punishment. Though these methods might seem basic by modern standards, they were essential at the time, demonstrating an evolving sense of police responsibilities.

Codes, Contracts, and Civil Law

Beyond criminal matters, early city-states recognized the need for enforcement in civil disputes. This included disagreements over land boundaries, debts, and business contracts. As trade and commerce grew, contractual arrangements became more complex. Merchants wanted reassurance that their deals would be honored and that, if not, the city's government would step in to enforce fairness.

For instance, in ancient Sumerian city-states, we find clay tablets detailing business transactions, loans, and the resolution of disputes. A city official or scribe would record the agreement, then store the tablet in a temple or government building. If one party later accused the other of not fulfilling the agreement, an official or judge could consult the tablet. If wrongdoing was found, the city-state had methods for restitution—seizing property, imposing fines, or forcing the guilty party to pay compensation. Guard-like officials might accompany the judge or scribe to ensure compliance if the accused tried to resist.

Such processes show the rising sophistication in the interplay between lawmaking, judicial proceedings, and enforcement. Rather than leaving everything to personal vendettas or clan-based feuds, city-states aimed to centralize the resolution of disputes, which in turn reinforced their authority.

Influence of Trade Networks on Policing

City-states that participated heavily in trade networks—like the Phoenicians or certain Greek polis (plural of polis, meaning city-state)—faced unique policing challenges. Wealth from trade attracted pirates, bandits, and other criminals. Ships at sea could be raided, caravans ambushed, and merchants robbed. Therefore, city-states that relied on trade had to extend their policing efforts beyond the city walls, patrolling trade routes, ports, and maritime lanes.

For maritime city-states, navies often doubled as policing forces at sea. They would clear waters of pirates, enforce tariffs, and protect merchant vessels. On land, certain city-states built watchtowers along key roads to deter bandits. In cases where these tactics were not enough, city-states might form alliances—agreeing to help one another capture criminals or share information about dangerous individuals. These early attempts at inter-city cooperation hint at how policing would later become a more unified effort across larger regions and nations.

Social Classes and Inequality in Policing

Like the ancient civilizations explored in Chapter 1, city-states also had hierarchical social structures. Often, the aristocracy or a group of wealthy families held the most power. They could influence the laws and punishments in ways that favored them. For example, a crime against a wealthy merchant might carry a heavier penalty than the same crime against a poor farmer. Similarly, the wealthy could afford to pay bribes or fines, while the poor might face harsher consequences for lack of resources.

This inequality naturally extended to policing. Guard forces were sometimes directed to protect the homes and goods of the rich more diligently, leaving lower-class neighborhoods with less security. Discontent could build among poorer citizens if they felt that "justice" primarily served the elite. In some city-states, this tension contributed to political reforms. For instance, Athens went through several reforms in its early history, aiming to balance power among social classes, at least to a degree. The idea was that a better sense of fairness in law enforcement would result in fewer uprisings and a more stable city.

Early Philosophical Views on Law and Order

One distinctive feature of certain city-states, especially in ancient Greece, was the philosophical debate about laws, justice, and governance. Thinkers like Plato and Aristotle wrote about the best ways to structure a society, including how to manage crime and wrongdoing. While these philosophical writings were not official law codes, they influenced how city-states thought about governance. Aristotle, for instance, discussed the role of virtue and the importance of a middle class in stabilizing society, implying that fair enforcement of laws was a key to harmony.

Even if philosophical views did not translate directly into immediate changes in policing, they left a mark on future generations of lawmakers. Over time, the idea that laws and their enforcement should reflect a notion of justice (rather than mere enforcement of power) would gain traction. This development laid groundwork for the more formalized and, in some cases, more democratic systems of policing that would emerge much later.

City-States Beyond the Mediterranean: The Indus Valley and Mesoamerica

While ancient Mesopotamia and Greece are often highlighted in discussions of city-states, other regions also witnessed the rise of urban centers with their own forms of policing. For example:

- **Indus Valley Civilization (c. 3300–1300 BCE):** Centered around cities like Mohenjo-daro and Harappa, it featured well-planned streets, advanced drainage systems, and a form of urban organization that hints at some level of social control. Though we lack explicit records of their policing methods, the uniformity in brick sizes and city layouts suggests a centralized authority that likely had officials ensuring rules were followed in construction, sanitation, and perhaps market trade.
- **Mesoamerican City-States:** In regions that are now Mexico and Central America, civilizations like the Maya developed city-states. Rulers, often seen as divine kings, maintained order through a combination of religious authority, military might, and officials who handled daily disputes. Large-scale building projects like pyramids and ceremonial centers required control over laborers, indicating some form of forced compliance that might have been enforced by specialized guards or soldiers.

These city-states, though geographically distant from the Mediterranean, shared core challenges: how to manage large populations, how to protect trade, and how to enforce the will of the ruling class. Their solutions likewise involved employing officials—whether they were scribes, guards, soldiers, or priestly administrators—to oversee and maintain order.

Transitioning from Volunteer to Paid Forces

Another milestone in the evolution of policing during this era was the gradual shift from volunteer or part-time enforcers to paid, professional ones. In many early city-states, citizens might be required to serve as watchmen for a specified period each year, or they might be called upon during emergencies. Over time, however, city leaders recognized the advantages of having people whose primary job was maintaining order. Paying these individuals from city coffers (which came from taxes and trade revenues) led to better performance and accountability.

Professionalization also meant that certain city-states could implement training routines, standard equipment, and a chain of command. A new recruit might learn how to recognize certain types of lawbreakers, how to respond to group violence, and how to handle tasks like guarding prisoners. While still nowhere near as regimented as modern police academies, these beginnings pointed toward more organized structures. The presence of a paid force also let city rulers keep a closer eye on potential corruption: salaries could help reduce the temptation to accept bribes (though it did not eliminate corruption entirely).

Civic Duty and Public Participation

Despite the rise of paid enforcement roles, public participation did not disappear. Many city-states saw policing as a collective effort. Citizens were expected to report crimes or help stop lawbreakers if they happened upon a crime in progress. The idea that "the people" had a stake in maintaining order contributed to a sense of shared responsibility, at least among the free, male population in places like ancient Athens. Women, slaves, and foreign residents were often excluded from these civic duties, reflecting broader social inequalities.

In certain situations, this public involvement made policing more efficient. If an armed guard or small team needed help apprehending a violent criminal, they could call upon bystanders. Conversely, the reliance on citizen involvement could sometimes lead to mob justice, where a crowd might decide an offender's fate on the spot. This tension between orderly enforcement by officials and chaotic vigilante actions was a recurring theme in many historical societies.

Legacy of the Early City-State Policing Models

By the time city-states were well established across regions like the Mediterranean, the Middle East, and beyond, the framework for policing was much more recognizable than in the simple tribal systems that preceded them. The distinguishing features of city-state policing included:

- **Formalized Roles and Hierarchies**: Clear lines of authority, from lawmakers to guards.
- **Focus on Public Spaces**: Enforcement of order in markets, festivals, and city gates.
- **Written Laws and Records**: Use of inscriptions, tablets, or early codifications to guide enforcement.
- **Combination of Military and Civil Duties**: Soldiers often handling tasks that we associate with police today.
- **Growing Professionalism**: A shift from volunteer watch systems to paid or semi-professional forces.
- **Importance of Public Compliance**: Reliance on citizen reporting and involvement to bolster official efforts.

City-states set important precedents for larger political entities that followed. When kings or emperors later united multiple city-states into kingdoms or empires, they often adopted or adapted existing local systems of policing. The success of city-states at creating order, handling disputes, and regulating commerce demonstrated the importance of structured law enforcement. Whether these efforts were truly fair or deeply biased in favor of elites, they paved the way for more advanced policing institutions.

Chapter 3

Order and Security in Ancient Rome

In the first two chapters, we examined how early forms of policing emerged in ancient societies and city-states, including the importance of written laws, watchmen, and guard systems. Now we turn our attention to **Ancient Rome**, one of history's most influential civilizations in the field of governance, law, and order. The Roman Empire's structure had a long-lasting effect on the Western world. By studying how Rome organized its guards, watch units, and policing functions, we can understand how future societies learned from and adapted those methods.

This chapter will cover several aspects of Roman order-keeping. We will look at how policing roles evolved during the Roman Republic and then under the Roman Empire. We will also discuss the distinct groups responsible for public safety—such as the **Vigiles**, **Urban Cohorts**, and the **Praetorian Guard**—and how each had a unique function. In addition, we will see how Roman law emphasized written statutes, administrative control, and a legal code that influenced many legal systems around the world in later centuries.

1. The Roman Republic and Early Policing

Rome did not begin as a massive empire. It started as a small settlement near the Tiber River, growing into a kingdom and later becoming a republic in 509 BCE. During the Roman Republic, power rested in elected officials such as consuls and senators. The city of Rome expanded its territories by conquest and alliances, gradually taking over the Italian peninsula and beyond.

In these early stages, **public order** was partly maintained by officials known as **magistrates**. Two notable magistrates were:

1. **Consuls** – The highest elected officials, with broad authority, including military command and administrative duties. They could call upon citizens to form a militia to handle emergencies or riots.
2. **Praetors** – Responsible for the administration of justice, including judicial functions. They supervised courts, handled lawsuits, and ensured that laws were followed.

Ordinary policing tasks—like stopping fights or dealing with theft—were not always carried out by special officers. Rather, the job often fell to local officials or private individuals who had some responsibility for their neighborhoods. In some parts of Rome, there was a system similar to "watch and ward," where a group of citizens would patrol their district. However, these groups were not well-organized, and enforcement was often inconsistent.

Additionally, Roman society placed significant weight on family honor and private legal actions. If a person committed a crime against another, the victim's family could pursue the matter through the courts. The state generally stepped in for major crimes such as treason or cases that threatened the city's stability.

As Rome's population and territory grew during the Republic, conflicts and unrest became more common. Streets became crowded, and disputes could quickly escalate. When riots broke out—often triggered by food shortages, political struggles, or the introduction of controversial laws—leaders sometimes had to use the city's militia or call on legions stationed nearby. This method of crowd control was far from ideal. It made clear that the city needed a permanent, well-organized approach to policing.

2. Transition to Empire and New Demands for Order

By the end of the first century BCE, internal conflicts had severely weakened the Republic. Leaders like Julius Caesar and Pompey fought for power, culminating in civil wars. Eventually, Caesar's adopted heir, **Octavian** (later named Augustus), took control. In 27 BCE, the Senate granted him extraordinary powers, and Rome officially became an empire, with Augustus as its first emperor.

With the rise of the empire, the central government gained stronger authority over the population. The emperors recognized that keeping the peace in Rome itself was vital for stability. If the capital city was chaotic, it would undermine the emperor's image and potentially encourage rebellions in the provinces. Thus, Emperor Augustus introduced reforms to create permanent policing and firefighting units in the city of Rome.

3. The Vigiles: Rome's First Organized Firefighters and Watchmen

Perhaps the most well-known of Augustus's new institutions were the **Vigiles**, established around 6 CE. The name "Vigiles" roughly translates to "watchmen," but these men also served as **firefighters**. Fires were a serious threat in Rome, a city crowded with wooden structures, narrow streets, and multi-story apartment houses (insulae). Augustus realized that an organized firefighting force would also be useful for law enforcement, especially at night, when much of the city was unguarded.

Structure and Duties

- The Vigiles were divided into **cohorts**, with each cohort assigned to a specific region of the city.
- Their primary job was to watch for fires, respond quickly, and contain them. Since water pumps were basic, the Vigiles relied on simpler tools such as buckets, axes, and blankets.
- Beyond fighting fires, the Vigiles acted as a night watch: patrolling streets, confronting petty criminals, and detaining suspects until they could be turned over to the city authorities.
- Over time, the Vigiles gained the authority to handle minor offenses on the spot, such as breaking up fights or chasing thieves caught in the act.

Importance and Impact

- By patrolling during the night, the Vigiles filled a gap in Rome's security. Before, citizens had little protection after dark.
- Their presence helped reduce common street crimes and provided a first response to emergencies.
- Although primarily a firefighting force, their dual role meant they were, in essence, **Rome's closest equivalent to a public police force**.

The Vigiles reported to the **Prefect of the Vigiles**, an official appointed by the emperor. This meant they were under direct imperial control, enabling the emperor to influence policing across the city. The direct link between the Vigiles and imperial authority reduced corruption in theory, though bribes and favoritism still occurred in practice.

4. The Urban Cohorts: Policing the Streets by Day

While the Vigiles handled night patrols and fires, daytime security fell to other units, notably the **Urban Cohorts** (Cohortes Urbanae). Established by Augustus to maintain order in Rome and later in other large cities of the empire, these cohorts functioned somewhat like a city-based military police.

Structure and Role

- The Urban Cohorts were commanded by the **Urban Prefect**, a high-ranking officer who also wielded judicial powers.
- Each cohort consisted of hundreds of well-trained soldiers. They wore armor similar to legionaries but typically did not go to war outside the city.
- Their job included controlling riots, preventing street violence, and assisting with major events where large crowds gathered.
- They could act with significant force if needed, stepping in to quell disturbances that the Vigiles could not handle alone.

Differences from the Vigiles

- The Urban Cohorts were more military in nature. They carried standard Roman military equipment and trained for crowd control and anti-riot tactics.
- They focused on daytime policing and large-scale public order, while the Vigiles specialized in night watch duties and firefighting.
- If a serious threat emerged, the Urban Cohorts could quickly call on assistance from the **Praetorian Guard** (discussed below) or even legionary detachments stationed near the city.

By establishing the Urban Cohorts, the emperor signaled that Rome's streets were a priority for the government. This allowed the empire to show strength to its citizens and, at the same time, reduce the number of violent uprisings that had plagued the late Republic.

5. The Praetorian Guard: Protectors of the Emperor

When discussing Roman order and security, one cannot ignore the **Praetorian Guard**. Initially, Roman generals used personal bodyguards known as "praetorian" units, but Augustus formalized this concept. The Praetorian Guard was an elite group of soldiers charged with protecting the emperor and his family. Although their primary purpose was not policing in the way we think of the term, they played a crucial role in maintaining power in Rome.

Duties and Power

- They guarded the imperial palace, accompanied the emperor during public appearances, and secured other important officials.
- Because they were the elite military force stationed in or near Rome, they had the means to influence political events. At times, they supported or toppled emperors.
- If there was a dire threat to the city, they could be deployed to assist the Urban Cohorts, although this was less common.

Influence on Policing

- The presence of the Praetorian Guard meant the emperor always had a loyal force at hand, which contributed to a sense of order—no one wanted to provoke the emperor's private army.
- Some emperors used the Guard to root out political rivals or to suppress dissent, which in effect made them a secret police force at times.
- Though separate from the day-to-day policing performed by the Vigiles and Urban Cohorts, the Guard shaped how the entire city approached crime and political opposition, as their authority overshadowed all others.

Over time, the Praetorian Guard became extremely powerful, occasionally acting like "kingmakers." Their power sometimes destabilized the empire, proving that having a strong policing or security force centered around a single leader could be a double-edged sword.

6. Provincial Policing: Governors and Local Forces

The city of Rome was the empire's heart, but vast territories extended into Europe, Africa, and Asia. Policing these far-flung provinces required a different approach. Emperors appointed **provincial governors** (variously called legati, proconsuls, propraetors, etc.) to rule on their behalf. These governors had the responsibility of maintaining law and order in their assigned regions.

Methods of Provincial Control

1. **Local Militia and Auxiliaries:** Each province could raise local troops to handle bandits, revolts, or public unrest. The Roman legions were usually stationed at critical points—like borders or trouble-prone areas—to respond to major threats.
2. **Romanization of Laws:** The governors, along with local elites, promoted Roman law, encouraging uniform legal structures. This helped unify policing and judicial processes across the empire.
3. **Tax Collection and Roads:** A key part of policing was ensuring safe trade and travel. Roman roads, patrolled by soldiers or local watchmen, allowed merchants to move goods with a reduced risk of robbery.

Collaboration with Local Elites

- In many regions, Rome allowed local kings, magistrates, or tribal leaders to remain in power, provided they acknowledged Roman authority. These leaders often maintained their own local policing methods, incorporating Roman practices as needed.
- Larger cities in the provinces sometimes had institutions similar to the Urban Cohorts or Vigiles, though these varied greatly based on local tradition and resources.

This decentralized approach meant that not all provinces had the same style of policing, but a broad Roman framework tied them together. The empire's emphasis on order, roads, and law helped reduce conflicts and encouraged commerce.

7. Courts, Laws, and the Role of Policing in Roman Justice

Roman law was a cornerstone of the empire's governance. Starting with the **Twelve Tables** in the mid-fifth century BCE, the Romans had a tradition of codifying statutes and legal principles. Over centuries, these laws developed into complex systems that addressed property rights, contracts, family matters, and criminal offenses. Policemen—whether they were Vigiles, Urban Cohorts, or local officials—were expected to enforce these laws and support judicial processes.

Basic Legal Principles

- **Public Law vs. Private Law:** Public law involved crimes against the state (like treason), and private law dealt with disputes between individuals. Policing touched both areas when apprehending suspects or ensuring compliance with court rulings.
- **Presumption of Status, Not Always Innocence:** Wealthy or high-status individuals often received preferential treatment, but the legal system aimed to formalize procedures to avoid blatant abuses.
- **Accusatorial System:** Much of Roman justice worked on an accusatorial basis, meaning a victim or accuser brought charges against a defendant. Officials would then handle trials if the case was serious enough.

Enforcement Process

- If someone was accused of a crime, a magistrate could order that person to appear in court. In Rome, the Urban Cohorts might assist in detaining suspects if they resisted.
- For civil matters, litigants mostly resolved disputes in front of a judge or praetor. However, if a losing party refused to pay damages, the authorities—possibly under the governor's direction in the provinces—could seize property or apply other penalties.
- As time passed, emperors issued edicts that further expanded or clarified the roles of local enforcers, standardizing procedures in different parts of the empire.

Roman law's structure would become a legacy that shaped medieval and modern legal systems. Policing was integral to this system because, without officials to ensure compliance, the best laws in the world would hold little force.

8. Crime and Punishments in Roman Society

Criminal offenses in Rome ranged from theft and assault to forgery, fraud, and murder. Punishments varied according to the nature of the crime, the status of the criminal, and the era. Roman society was hierarchical, so a senator might face a different penalty than a commoner for the same offense, though reforms tried to limit such disparities.

Common Punishments

1. **Fines:** Frequently used for minor crimes, especially among the wealthy who could afford them.
2. **Forced Labor or Hard Labor:** Offenders might be sent to work in mines or on large agricultural estates.
3. **Exile:** Rome often punished political troublemakers by banishing them from the city or a certain province.
4. **Execution:** Reserved for serious crimes like treason or repeated offenses. Methods of execution included beheading for citizens (considered more "honorable") and crucifixion for slaves or non-citizens.
5. **Public Shaming:** Lower-level punishments sometimes included public flogging or humiliation.

The job of the policing units was to apprehend suspects, keep them in custody if necessary, and ensure they faced the relevant judicial proceedings. In large riots or conspiracies, the Urban Cohorts and even the Praetorian Guard could be involved, making arrests and carrying out swift punishments under the emperor's decree.

9. Provincial Challenges: Banditry, Rebellions, and Frontier Security

Beyond the city of Rome, maintaining order in the vast empire required tackling unique problems:

1. **Banditry and Highway Robbery:** Though Roman roads were famously well-constructed, remote stretches could still harbor bandits. Soldiers or local watch units patrolled these routes, but the empire's extensive network meant total control was difficult.
2. **Rebellions:** Some regions resisted Roman rule, either out of loyalty to local customs or in reaction to heavy taxation. Policing in these cases went beyond everyday enforcement; it involved crushing revolts. Emperors might dispatch legions to restore order, after which local policing forces kept watch for new signs of discontent.
3. **Frontier Posts:** On the empire's borders—along the Rhine, Danube, or in distant deserts—Roman forts guarded entry points. Soldiers stationed there also acted as law enforcers for nearby settlements. If trouble flared, these soldiers often had the final say in maintaining peace.

This blend of military action, local policing, and governance by Roman officials allowed the empire to remain fairly stable for centuries, despite its vast size.

10. Policing in the Later Empire and Decline

Over time, the Roman Empire changed its power structure. The capital shifted from Rome to other cities like Constantinople (formerly Byzantium), especially after Emperor Constantine embraced Christianity and reorganized the empire in the early 4th century CE. Administrative reforms altered how the provinces were managed, and the empire split into the **Western Roman Empire** and the **Eastern Roman Empire**.

In many areas, the well-organized systems of the earlier empire began to weaken. Military pressures, economic troubles, and invasions by groups such as the Visigoths and Vandals disrupted daily life. As central authority weakened, local magnates or warlords took on more policing functions. The famous units, such as the Urban Cohorts or the Vigiles, did not remain as strong or well-coordinated in later centuries.

Key Changes

- The Praetorian Guard's power fluctuated with political turmoil, and it was disbanded by Emperor Constantine in 312 CE, removing a long-standing yet at times destabilizing force in Rome.
- Urban Cohorts and Vigiles continued in some form but faced fewer resources. Civil strife, lack of funds, and constant external threats reduced their effectiveness.
- In the provinces, local landowners gained more influence, often protecting their tenants and estates through private militias rather than depending on imperial authorities.

These shifts signaled the end of a centrally controlled Roman policing system. While the Eastern Empire (Byzantine) would persist for nearly another millennium, its structure also evolved, developing new forms of security and military practices that were quite different from classical Rome's.

11. Legacy of Roman Policing

Despite Rome's eventual decline in the West, its example influenced many later societies. Among the most important contributions were:

1. **Organized Urban Forces:** Rome's division of roles—night watch (Vigiles), daytime riot control (Urban Cohorts), and elite protection (Praetorian Guard)—gave a model of specialized units performing policing tasks.
2. **Legal Codes:** Roman law deeply influenced medieval law in Europe. Many kingdoms adopted or adapted Roman legal principles, which, in turn, shaped how law enforcement was viewed.
3. **Infrastructure and Administration:** The emphasis on roads, record-keeping, and local oversight demonstrated the benefit of systematic administration for maintaining law and order.
4. **Imperial Authority:** The idea that a central ruler (emperor, king, or similar) could establish official policing systems was carried forward, helping future monarchies and governments see the value in structured enforcement.

The Roman Empire, through centuries of adaptation, showed how large-scale policing and administrative controls could function. Even though many of its specific institutions disappeared, the underlying concepts—organized patrols, fire watch, crowd control, and official structures for law enforcement—set a precedent.

Chapter 4

Medieval Policing in Europe

When the Western Roman Empire fell in the late 5th century CE, Europe entered a period often referred to as the **Middle Ages** or the **Medieval period**. This era continued roughly until the 15th century. The collapse of Roman central authority left a patchwork of successor kingdoms, tribal realms, and local lords, each with its own approach to governance and law enforcement. Without a strong imperial system, policing became more localized and often more informal.

In this chapter, we will explore how policing functioned in Europe during medieval times. We will discuss the **feudal system**, which tied land ownership to military service and had significant implications for law enforcement. We will look at the emergence of local officials like **sheriffs** and **bailiffs**, whose roles originated in the early medieval period, and we will examine community-based practices such as the **tithing** and **frankpledge** systems. Finally, we will consider how the Church influenced crime control and how knights, mercenaries, and royal retinues sometimes carried out policing tasks.

1. The Transition from Roman Rule to Feudal Kingdoms

After the Western Roman Empire's collapse, Germanic tribes, such as the **Visigoths**, **Ostrogoths**, **Franks**, and **Vandals**, established their own kingdoms in former Roman territories. The infrastructure, including roads and administrative institutions, did not vanish overnight but suffered from neglect and war damage.

Local Power Structures

- Wealth and authority became concentrated in the hands of local lords or warriors who could defend their land.
- These lords often ruled from fortified settlements or castles, providing security to nearby peasants in exchange for labor and loyalty.
- Royal authority, where it existed, was typically weak in the early medieval period, so kings depended on the support of influential nobles to maintain order in distant parts of their realms.

Impact on Policing

- Policing largely fell to local leaders who enforced laws as they saw fit.
- Armed retainers of a lord might double as enforcers, protecting the lord's interests and managing conflicts among peasants.
- Over time, some regions attempted to codify local or tribal laws, but enforcement remained inconsistent.

In many places, Roman law gave way to **customary law**—unwritten rules reflecting local traditions. If a dispute arose, local assemblies or courts, often presided over by a noble or a church official, heard the case. Enforcement of verdicts might require the presence of armed men loyal to that court or lord.

2. The Feudal System and Its Effect on Law Enforcement

Under feudalism, the king (or top monarch) was technically the ultimate owner of all land, granting pieces of land—called **fiefs**—to nobles (vassals) in exchange for military service or financial dues. Those nobles, in turn, might grant parts of their land to lesser vassals, continuing a chain of obligation down to knights and peasants.

Duties and Obligations

1. **Military Service:** Vassals promised to provide armed knights or troops to the king when needed.
2. **Protection of Peasants:** Lords provided security within their domain, preventing raids or internal disturbances.
3. **Legal Authority:** Lords often had the right to hold **manorial courts** on their estates. They could fine or punish those under their jurisdiction for various offenses.

Because each lord managed his own land, policing did not operate from a single, central authority. Instead, local enforcers—often the lord's armed men—carried out commands. If a peasant committed a crime, they might be brought before the lord's court. The lord would act as both judge and policeman, deciding the verdict and punishment. This system could vary widely from one manor to the next, with fairness depending on the lord's temperament.

3. Community-Based Policing: Tithings and the Frankpledge System

While feudal lords played a huge role in law enforcement, not all policing was top-down. In some parts of medieval Europe, especially in Anglo-Saxon England, there were forms of **community-based policing**. These systems relied on the collective responsibility of ordinary people to maintain order. Two related concepts stand out:

1. **Tithings**
    - A tithing was a group of about ten households. Every man aged twelve or older was required to join a tithing.
    - If someone in the tithing committed a crime, the others were responsible for bringing him to justice. Failure to do so could result in collective punishments or fines for the entire tithing.
    - This approach created peer pressure to follow the law. People were less likely to hide a criminal if they knew they could all be punished for it.
2. **Frankpledge**
    - An evolution of the tithing system, the frankpledge required groups of households (usually ten tithings, known collectively as a "hundred" in some areas) to keep the peace.
    - A leader or chief was chosen to oversee the group, ensuring that members upheld their communal duties.
    - Regular meetings, known as **view of frankpledge**, allowed local authorities to verify that everyone was in a tithing and that suspects were accounted for.

These community-based practices helped reduce petty crime, as criminals had nowhere to hide if entire neighborhoods were accountable for turning them in. However, the systems also had weaknesses. If a community was reluctant to turn on one of its own, crimes could go unpunished.

4. The Sheriff and the Shire System

In England, the concept of the **sheriff** (originally **"shire-reeve"**) became a significant element of medieval policing. A shire was a regional division similar to a county. The king appointed a shire-reeve to oversee the shire, collect taxes, and maintain law and order in the king's name.

Duties of the Sheriff

1. **Tax Collection:** Ensuring that the crown received its due revenues.
2. **Organizing the Local Posse:** If a crime occurred, or if the sheriff needed help chasing a criminal, he could call upon the **posse comitatus**—all able-bodied men in the area—to help.
3. **Attending Royal Courts:** The sheriff might oversee local trials or bring accused criminals to royal judges.
4. **Maintaining the King's Peace:** The idea of the king's peace meant that crimes were offenses not only against the victim but also against royal authority.

Because the sheriff was the king's direct representative, his role was more official and centralized than the feudal lord's. Over time, this position expanded in importance, influencing other areas of Europe, although under different titles and organizational structures.

5. Manorial Courts and Local Justice

At the lowest level, the **manorial court** governed peasants who lived and worked on a lord's estate. This court dealt with everyday disputes: boundary disagreements, unpaid rents, petty theft, and breaches of local customs. The lord or a steward presided, and villagers might serve as witnesses or jury members. Punishments could involve fines, additional work, or public humiliation.

In some cases, if a crime was severe—such as murder or major theft—the manorial court might pass the case upward to a higher authority, like the sheriff or a royal judge. This layered system meant there was a hierarchy of courts: local manors, shire or county courts, and eventually royal courts. Each level had policing officials who ensured that suspects appeared in court and that verdicts were carried out.

6. The Church's Influence on Medieval Policing

Throughout medieval Europe, the **Catholic Church** was a powerful institution, owning vast land and wielding spiritual authority over the population. The Church had its own legal system known as **canon law**, presided over by church officials. Certain offenses—like heresy, blasphemy, or moral failures by clergy—fell under the Church's jurisdiction rather than the secular courts.

Church Enforcement Methods

1. **Ecclesiastical Courts:** These courts handled disputes involving clergy or moral and religious matters. They could impose penances, excommunication, or other spiritual penalties.
2. **Sanctuary:** Churches offered sanctuary to accused persons. If a suspect fled inside a church, local enforcers were often prohibited from dragging them out by force. The suspect might negotiate a settlement or agree to exile.
3. **Monastic Police or Guards:** Some large monasteries maintained small armed forces to protect church lands from bandits or raiding lords.

This dual system—secular and ecclesiastical—sometimes caused disputes about who had jurisdiction. Church officials claimed that clergy should not be tried by secular courts, while kings and nobles often disagreed. Still, the Church was a central pillar of medieval life, and many people respected its role in maintaining social order.

7. Knights, Mercenaries, and the Use of Force

During the Middle Ages, knights represented the most visible symbol of military and protective power. Trained from youth in riding and combat, knights were sworn to uphold chivalric codes, ideally defending the weak and serving just causes. In practice, knights were also loyal to specific lords or kings, and their policing or protecting role often depended on whom they served.

Mercenaries were also common—hired soldiers who fought or performed enforcement duties for pay. A lord needing extra muscle to defend a castle or quell a revolt could recruit mercenaries, some of whom were notorious for violence or pillaging. The presence of mercenary forces sometimes blurred the line between legitimate policing and outright intimidation.

8. Bandits, Outlaws, and Robber Barons

The unstable nature of medieval politics, combined with limited centralized control, gave rise to **banditry** and the presence of "**robber barons**." These were nobles who used their castles or fortresses to control roads, charging illegal tolls or simply robbing passing merchants.

Efforts to Combat Banditry

- Sheriffs, or sometimes royal expeditions, attempted to destroy outlaw strongholds.
- Merchant guilds formed their own protective associations to hire guards for caravans.
- Some rulers passed "**peace and truce of God**" movements, trying to limit violence by establishing certain times or places where warfare or robbery was forbidden.

However, due to the feudal structure, local lords could be as problematic as the outlaws. A strong king might keep them in check, but weaker monarchs struggled to enforce national laws, leaving many regions at the mercy of local tyrants.

9. The Growth of Towns and Early Municipal Policing

Despite the feudal backdrop, the late medieval period witnessed the growth of **towns** and **cities**, fueled by trade and craft guilds. Some towns gained charters granting them the right to self-govern. Under these charters, townspeople could elect officials like **mayors**, **aldermen**, or **burghers** who oversaw local markets, trade regulations, and security.

Municipal Policing

1. **Town Watches:** Volunteers or paid watchmen patrolled city gates and streets, especially after dark. They would ring bells or raise alarms if they spotted suspicious activities.

2. **City Guards:** Larger towns might maintain small professional forces to guard walls and respond to criminal incidents.
3. **Guild Enforcement:** Craft and merchant guilds had their own rules and punishments for members who broke trade regulations or cheated customers, contributing to an early form of commercial policing.

These self-governing towns reduced the power of feudal lords within urban areas. As trade expanded, town-based law enforcement became more organized, laying groundwork for later municipal police forces in the early modern period.

10. Trials by Ordeal and the Influence on Policing

In the early Middle Ages, formal evidence-based trials were limited. Instead, many cultures used **trials by ordeal**—such as walking on hot coals, plunging a hand into boiling water, or retrieving a stone from a cauldron—to determine guilt or innocence. The belief was that God would protect an innocent person from harm.

Policing Angle

- Local enforcers or lords supervised these ordeals, ensuring the accused actually performed the test.
- If the ordeal indicated guilt, the community considered the offender justly punished or condemned.
- Over time, the Church and later medieval monarchs discouraged ordeals, favoring more rational evidence-based systems.

Though trials by ordeal eventually fell out of favor, they highlight the period's reliance on religious or mystical means rather than organized investigative policing.

11. Royal Justices and Itinerant Courts

From the 12th century onward in some regions, especially in England, kings began sending out **itinerant justices**—roving judges—to hold **assize courts**. These judges traveled from shire to shire, hearing serious cases and ensuring that the crown's law was enforced uniformly.

Contribution to Policing

- Sheriffs and local bailiffs were expected to gather juries and produce accused persons before these judges.
- Juries, composed of local men, provided information on suspected criminals, functioning as an early investigative body.
- Through these traveling courts, local policing and justice were tied more closely to the monarchy, slowly centralizing law enforcement.

In France and other parts of Europe, similar practices arose, with kings and princes trying to create more consistent legal systems. Over time, these royal initiatives reduced the power of local lords, shaping a more unified notion of "king's justice."

12. Weapons Control and Sumptuary Laws

Medieval authorities recognized that controlling weapons could reduce violence. Some kings issued decrees limiting who could carry swords or bows within city limits. Towns might ban certain weapons during festivals or market days to prevent brawls.

Similarly, **sumptuary laws**—rules governing how people dressed or displayed wealth—were sometimes used as a way to keep social order. While not strictly policing in the modern sense, enforcing these laws fell to local officials and constables. Their tasks included checking that citizens conformed to regulations about clothing, jewelry, or even the size of feasts, believing that excessive display could cause envy or riots.

13. Punishments, Public Spectacles, and Deterrence

Medieval Europe often used **public punishments** to deter crime. Stocks, pillories, and public floggings shamed offenders in the eyes of the community. Executions, when carried out, were sometimes treated as public events where the entire town might gather.

Role of Local Officials

- Constables, bailiffs, or watchmen brought the condemned to these punishment sites.
- The event served as a grim warning to others, reinforcing local authority and the seriousness of crime.

While these punishments could be brutal by modern standards, they were part of the medieval worldview, which accepted pain and public shame as legitimate forms of criminal justice.

14. The Influence of Chivalry and Moral Codes

Certain medieval societies valued a code of **chivalry**—idealizing knights who protected the innocent, upheld justice, and defended the church. In literary works, knights often acted like roving law enforcers, stepping in to right wrongs. Real knights, of course, were more concerned with serving their feudal lords and personal gain. Still, the romantic notion of knightly virtue had some impact, encouraging the idea that the powerful should protect the weak.

Additionally, moral codes tied to Christian teachings promoted the concept of charity, mercy, and the moral duty of rulers to safeguard their subjects. Some rulers made genuine efforts to improve local courts, quell lawlessness, and provide more consistent justice. Though progress was often slow and uneven, these beliefs gradually shaped public expectations.

15. Crusades and Their Effect on Policing

Between the 11th and 13th centuries, European knights and nobles participated in **Crusades** to the Holy Land. These large-scale movements had indirect effects on policing back home:

1. **Militarization of Society:** Many knights and warriors gained combat experience, bringing violent skills back to their homelands. This could lead to an increase in local conflicts.
2. **Military Orders:** Groups like the **Knights Templar** formed to protect pilgrims traveling to the Holy Land. Though their focus was abroad, they sometimes policed routes in Europe, too, especially in territories they controlled.
3. **Vacuum in Local Leadership:** With so many nobles absent, some communities took policing into their own hands or fell under the sway of opportunistic local powers.

While the Crusades were primarily religious and military campaigns, they did influence how certain regions in Europe approached law enforcement, especially in frontier or newly conquered areas.

16. Late Medieval Developments: The Growth of Monarchies

In the later medieval period (roughly 13th to 15th centuries), kings in countries like England, France, and Spain worked to centralize their power. They passed laws that applied across their kingdoms and appointed more official roles in local governance:

- **Bailiffs and Seneschals:** Appointed by the king or high nobles to manage estates and keep order, especially in France.
- **Justices of the Peace:** Emerged in England, with the power to judge minor offenses and maintain the king's peace in their region. They could call upon local constables to make arrests.
- **Professional Soldiers:** Monarchs increasingly hired standing armies or used professional retinues to quell rebellions or major criminal threats.

These shifts marked a gradual move away from purely feudal policing. Instead, the king's officials started to replace or regulate local lords' private forces.

17. Urban Militia and Guild Security

As urban centers grew wealthier, many towns maintained a **citizen militia**. On specific days, male citizens would practice archery or basic weapons handling. This militia could be mobilized to defend the city against external attacks or to maintain internal peace.

Guilds also contributed to local order by employing guards to protect trade fairs or ensure that merchants followed city regulations. Some guilds enforced their own disciplinary measures on members who broke rules, effectively acting as small-scale police within their commercial domain.

18. Corruption and the Struggle for Fair Enforcement

Medieval policing was not free from corruption. Sheriffs or bailiffs might misuse their authority, demanding bribes. Lords could abuse their judicial powers to punish rivals or enrich themselves. Moreover, biases against certain groups—like peasants, non-Christians, or foreigners—led to unequal treatment under the law.

Some monarchs, eager to limit abuses, issued decrees or charters requiring officials to treat subjects fairly, or at least follow prescribed procedures. The Magna Carta in England (1215) is a famous example, though it mostly served the interests of barons, it also contained language protecting freemen from unlawful detention, hinting at an early concept of due process.

19. Transition to Early Modern Policing in Late Medieval Times

By the end of the Middle Ages, the seeds for a more centralized policing system were planted. Larger kingdoms, stronger monarchies, and expanding trade networks encouraged better administration. Also, the intellectual climate of the later Middle Ages, leading into the Renaissance, began challenging traditional structures. People started to question arbitrary power and feudal obligations, though true reforms would take centuries to materialize fully.

Notable Trends

- The role of the sheriff or similar officials became more standardized in certain kingdoms.
- Towns continued refining their watch and ward systems, some paying professionals to patrol at night.
- The Church's judicial reach remained significant, but secular authorities increasingly asserted control over moral and religious offenses.

Chapter 5

The Rise of Sheriffs and Constables in Rural Communities

In the previous chapters, we discussed how policing took shape in ancient and medieval societies. We looked at major civilizations like Rome and surveyed the fragmented systems of the Middle Ages. Now we shift our focus to the growth of **sheriffs**, **constables**, and other local officers in rural communities, especially in England and parts of Europe. Though these roles existed in some form during the medieval period, they became more structured over time. Their evolution is critical to understanding how local policing laid the groundwork for more centralized systems in later centuries.

This chapter explores how the sheriff's office and the constable role emerged, how they functioned in rural life, and the ways they addressed common crimes, disputes, and social issues. We will also see how these positions adapted as kingdoms grew more powerful, how they handled everyday matters of law enforcement, and how they combined with or diverged from other local institutions and customs.

1. Origins of the Sheriff and Constable Roles

1.1. Sheriff (Shire-Reeve) in Early England

The title **"sheriff"** is derived from the Old English words for "shire" (a regional district, roughly analogous to a county) and "reeve" (a high-ranking local official). Tracing its roots to the Anglo-Saxon period before the Norman Conquest of England (1066), the sheriff's position was well established by the 11th century.

- **Royal Representative:** A sheriff primarily served as the king's representative in a shire. This role required collecting taxes, overseeing local justice, and making sure the king's decrees were enforced.
- **Keeping the Peace:** The notion of "keeping the king's peace" was a central idea in medieval English law. Crimes were treated not just as private wrongs but as offenses against royal authority. The sheriff was tasked with ensuring public order on the king's behalf.
- **Leading the Posse:** When a crime occurred, the sheriff could call upon the **posse comitatus**—all able-bodied men in the shire—to help pursue criminals or restore order during rebellions and uprisings.

Over the centuries, as monarchies in England fluctuated in strength, the sheriff's responsibilities also shifted. In some periods, sheriffs held vast powers, almost like local warlords. In other eras, strong kings curtailed sheriff authority to prevent them from becoming too influential.

1.2. The Rise of the Constable

While the sheriff operated at the county or shire level, the **constable** typically served at a more local or parish level. The exact origin of the term varies, but by the late medieval and early modern periods, constables in England (and similarly named roles in other parts of Europe) were recognized as vital enforcers of local justice.

- **Local Appointments:** Constables were often chosen by local officials, or in some areas, elected by parishioners. They were not always professionals; many were ordinary townspeople or villagers required to take on this duty for a set term, such as a year.
- **Everyday Policing:** A constable's work involved breaking up fights, making arrests for minor crimes, and ensuring that local bylaws were respected.
- **Supporting Higher Authorities:** In more serious matters, constables assisted sheriffs, traveling judges, or other royal officials by delivering suspects to higher courts.

By the 15th and 16th centuries, the roles of sheriff and constable became more defined in England's statutory law, shaping a pattern that would later spread via British influence to other parts of the world.

2. Roles and Responsibilities in Daily Life

2.1. Collecting Taxes and Dues

One of the sheriff's primary duties remained the collection of taxes for the crown or local nobility. This task was vital because medieval and early modern governments relied on taxes to fund armies, maintain roads, and support royal courts. Sheriffs oversaw the process at the county level, coordinating with bailiffs or lower-ranked officials who dealt with individual parishes.

Constables also became involved in tax collection, though usually in a supportive capacity. When a community was slow to pay, the constable might deliver warnings or assist in seizing property to satisfy debts. This responsibility could make local enforcers unpopular, especially during poor harvests or economic downturns.

2.2. Arrests, Warrants, and Summons

Sheriffs issued **warrants** and **summons** when the king's court or local justices ordered someone to appear before them. Constables, being closer to the people, executed these warrants: they located individuals, made arrests if necessary, and escorted suspects to the appropriate court.

In some regions, the constable was also responsible for managing a local **lock-up** or holding cell. When a suspect was caught, the constable housed them overnight or until the sheriff's men arrived. This arrangement allowed for a continuous flow of suspects from the local to the higher authority level, ensuring that the justice system functioned.

2.3. Public Order, Fights, and Brawls

Rural communities often witnessed disputes over land boundaries, livestock, or inheritance. A simple disagreement between neighbors could escalate into a fight involving extended families. The constable, as the local enforcer, might step in to break it up. If the dispute continued, the sheriff or a royal judge might intervene.

In market towns, a constable's job during fair days was crucial. Large gatherings drew in traders, travelers, and sometimes petty criminals. By patrolling the marketplace and responding to theft or disorder, constables tried to keep commerce running smoothly.

3. The Frankpledge System and Local Watch

3.1. Overlap with Community Responsibility

From our discussion in Chapter 4, we learned about the **frankpledge** system (or tithing groups) where male inhabitants were mutually responsible for each other's conduct. This community-based policing approach often overlapped with the roles of sheriffs and constables. For instance, if someone in a tithing failed to appear before a local court, the sheriff might hold the entire group accountable. The constable would collaborate with tithing leaders to ensure suspects were produced.

3.2. Watch and Ward

In medieval and early modern towns, the **watch and ward** system required local men to stand guard during designated hours, especially at night or during festivals. Constables oversaw scheduling and enforcement—making sure citizens fulfilled their watch duties or found a substitute. If a watchman spotted trouble, he would sound an alarm (sometimes by ringing a bell or a "hue and cry"), prompting others to join in pursuit of criminals.

This method was basic but effective for small rural communities where everyone knew one another. The sheriff would typically become involved only if the crime was serious or if the culprits escaped local capture.

4. Changing Power Dynamics: Royal Authority vs. Local Autonomy

4.1. The Crown's Efforts to Centralize

As European monarchies grew stronger, kings and queens sought to reduce the power of local nobility. They did this by passing laws that more clearly defined the duties of sheriffs and constables, ensuring these officers answered directly to the crown.

- **Statutes and Reforms:** England, for example, saw the passing of statutes that required sheriffs to reside in their shires, keep detailed records, and submit regular reports to the royal administration.
- **Limiting Abuses:** There was a concern that sheriffs might misuse their power, terrorizing peasants or favoring friends. New regulations attempted to check corruption by setting fines or punishments for officials who overstepped.

4.2. Tensions with Nobles and Gentry

Local lords sometimes resented these attempts at centralization. They preferred a situation where their private forces or stewards handled disputes without royal interference. In certain regions, conflicts arose between royal-appointed sheriffs and noble families who had grown accustomed to running their lands as mini-kingdoms.

Constables also felt these tensions. Some were appointed by local lords, while others were recognized by the crown. Their loyalties might be divided, especially when a noble's wishes clashed with royal directives. Over time, many nobility adjusted to the new realities, forging alliances with the crown to maintain partial autonomy while respecting official channels.

5. Everyday Crimes and Their Policing in Rural Areas

5.1. Poaching and Game Laws

One of the most common rural crimes was **poaching**. Landed gentry and aristocrats considered game animals (deer, boar, rabbits, etc.) on their estates to be private property. Hunting these animals without permission was a serious offense.

- **Sheriff Involvement:** In cases of large-scale poaching rings or organized gangs, a sheriff might organize a posse to catch them.
- **Constable Involvement:** On a day-to-day level, constables responded to complaints from estate managers or local farmers who suspected trespassers. Constables could search a suspect's home for illegal game or weapons used for hunting.

Punishments for poaching varied, but could include fines, public humiliation, or, in severe cases, imprisonment. Over time, strict **game laws** turned poaching into a major source of tension between peasants and landowners.

5.2. Vagrancy and Beggars

Rural communities also worried about **vagrants**—individuals or families traveling with no fixed home or occupation. In an age without robust social welfare, beggars often roamed the countryside, seeking alms or odd jobs. Local authorities feared that vagrants could be thieves or potential troublemakers.

- **Constables' Role:** They were expected to confront suspicious wanderers, check their backgrounds, and sometimes escort them out of the area if they lacked legitimate business.
- **Sheriff's Oversight:** If a vagrant caused repeated problems, the sheriff might detain them, awaiting a traveling judge who could decide their fate.

This approach to vagrancy reflected the era's anxiety about outsiders and the desire of local leaders to maintain social order. People with no ties to the land were seen as potential criminals in the making.

5.3. Moral and Social Offenses

Local officials also enforced community standards regarding moral behavior. While the Church had its own courts, secular officers sometimes detained individuals for public drunkenness, fighting, or adultery if it caused public disorder. In many communities, these weren't always seen as purely private matters; they threatened social harmony.

Constables might break up gatherings deemed inappropriate, such as rowdy late-night tavern gatherings. They could also deliver admonitions or fines. In more extreme cases, they turned the matter over to the sheriff if a larger investigation was required.

6. Tools and Methods of Enforcement

6.1. Basic Weapons and Authority

Sheriffs and constables in rural Europe were rarely outfitted with elaborate uniforms. Instead, they carried symbols of their office, such as a **staff** or **rod**, or in some places a **badge** to display their authority. Weapons might include swords, daggers, or clubs, though these varied by region and era.

Because these officers were typically part-time or came from within the community, their effectiveness depended heavily on personal relationships and reputation. A well-respected constable found it easier to de-escalate conflicts, while a disliked one might struggle to command respect.

6.2. The Role of Community Witnesses

Investigations were rudimentary. If a crime took place, the sheriff or constable might gather **witnesses** to piece together the facts. Although there were no formal detective units, local knowledge was a powerful resource. Villagers who knew each other could quickly identify suspicious newcomers or note if someone was acting out of character.

In some parts of Europe, local law required every able-bodied man to respond to a **"hue and cry"**—the loud call for help when a crime was discovered. Refusal to join in the chase could lead to fines or accusations of aiding criminals. This communal approach often forced criminals to flee long distances to avoid capture, since neighboring villages would also join the pursuit.

6.3. Record-Keeping and Communication

Sheriffs were often required to maintain **rolls** or lists of suspects, fines, and the outcomes of local court sessions. These records could be submitted to higher authorities or traveling judges. This practice helped standardize law enforcement by linking rural communities to the broader legal system.

Communication among villages and towns was slow by modern standards. Messengers on horseback or foot carried letters and warrants. When time was critical—such as pursuing dangerous criminals—officials relied more on the hue and cry system than on sending formal communications.

7. Expansion of the Sheriff-Constable Model

7.1. Influence Beyond England

Although the term "sheriff" is most famously associated with England, similar positions existed elsewhere in Europe. In France, the **sénéchal** or **bailli** had comparable duties, and in parts of Germany, the **Vogt** or **Amtmann** served a similar function. Each role mixed administrative, judicial, and law enforcement responsibilities, often reflecting the local feudal hierarchy.

By the late medieval and early modern period, many of these officers fell under tighter royal or princely control, mirroring England's trend. Whether called sheriff, bailli, or Vogt, these officials managed local policing, tax collection, and acted as the monarchy's face in rural communities.

7.2. Colonial Offshoots

Later, as European powers expanded overseas, they transplanted elements of the sheriff-constable system to their colonies. In the Americas, for instance, English colonists appointed sheriffs in early settlements. These sheriffs played roles similar to their English counterparts, bridging local self-governance and the distant authority of the crown.

Though colonization is a topic we will explore more deeply in Chapter 8, it is worth noting that the rural policing model—centered on a chief local enforcer—proved adaptable in new territories, especially where scattered farms and small towns needed practical, decentralized law enforcement.

8. Challenges and Criticisms

8.1. Corruption and Abuse of Power

Sheriffs and constables, given their ability to levy fines, collect taxes, and enforce the law, sometimes succumbed to corruption. A sheriff might demand excessive fees or bribes. Constables could misuse their position to settle personal grudges. Over time, monarchs and parliaments introduced regulations to punish corrupt officials, but enforcement was inconsistent.

In some cases, local communities pushed back by complaining to higher authorities or refusing to comply with corrupt demands. These disputes occasionally escalated into violent confrontations, especially if a sheriff tried to seize property or jail respected community members.

8.2. Lack of Professional Training

For most of the medieval and early modern periods, neither sheriffs nor constables received systematic training. Their knowledge came from tradition, local statutes, and whatever personal experience they gained on the job. While many did their duties responsibly, others struggled with complex legal cases, especially if literacy levels were low.

Calls for better training grew louder in the 17th and 18th centuries, setting the stage for the more professional police systems that would emerge in the 19th century. However, that shift lay in the future; for the era we are discussing, law enforcement remained a patchwork of local customs and personal abilities.

8.3. Varying Degrees of Effectiveness

Rural policing could be quite effective at suppressing petty crime when communities worked together. However, it often faltered against organized or powerful criminals, especially if they had noble patrons or if they roamed from one county to another. Sheriffs lacked the resources to track criminals over long distances, and communication delays between shires could allow offenders to escape.

Despite these challenges, the sheriff and constable system remained the cornerstone of local law enforcement for centuries. Its resilience lay in how deeply it was tied to rural life and social structures. People recognized that, while flawed, this system provided a measure of stability and protection in a world where travel was dangerous and centralized authority often far away.

9. Cultural and Social Impacts of Local Policing

9.1. Reinforcing Social Hierarchies

Sheriffs and constables were usually selected from the ranks of the socially powerful or well-established. This meant that law enforcement roles often reinforced existing hierarchies. Landowners and local elites had a say in who became constable, which sometimes led to bias in arrests and prosecutions.

For instance, a wealthy farmer accused of a minor offense might receive lenient treatment from the sheriff, who was also the farmer's friend or business partner. Conversely, a poor laborer with no social connections might face harsher penalties for similar conduct. These inequities mirrored broader social structures of the time.

9.2. Community Cohesion and Dispute Resolution

On the other hand, the fact that constables and sheriffs were local (or at least lived within the same region) could foster **community cohesion**. When a respected figure was chosen, residents were more likely to comply peacefully with law enforcement. Communities often resolved small disputes among themselves, involving the constable only when necessary.

Festivals, market days, and religious gatherings sometimes brought the community together to discuss local issues. Sheriffs, if they were in attendance, might use the occasion to hear grievances or reinforce the king's authority. This blending of community tradition and official power played a part in maintaining order without requiring a large standing force.

10. Evolving into the Early Modern Period

10.1. The Tudor Era in England

A notable example of the changing role of sheriffs and constables can be seen in **Tudor England** (late 15th to early 17th century). Under monarchs like Henry VIII and Elizabeth I, the crown worked to strengthen royal authority. Statutes clarified how sheriffs and constables should be appointed, their legal powers, and their responsibilities to the crown.

Simultaneously, **Justices of the Peace** (JPs) gained more importance, hearing minor cases and ensuring local order. Sheriffs and constables collaborated with JPs, creating an early network of rural law enforcement and judiciary roles. This period showed how local policing was gradually woven into a more centralized legal fabric.

10.2. Legislative Reforms

Across Europe, different regions passed legislation that shaped how local enforcers operated. Some laws aimed to standardize the process of arrests, define bail conditions, and clarify how criminals should be handed over to higher courts. Others addressed specific issues such as vagrancy, hunting rights, or highway robbery.

These reforms often aimed to balance local autonomy with the need for overarching stability. While local officers retained on-the-ground authority, they increasingly acted within a framework of national laws, bridging the gap between the crown and ordinary citizens.

Chapter 6

Policing Systems in Eastern Empires

While Chapters 1 through 5 have largely focused on the Mediterranean world, medieval Europe, and the rise of local policing roles in rural communities, law enforcement in other parts of the globe followed distinct trajectories. During the medieval and early modern periods (and even earlier), vast empires in the East—ranging from the Islamic Caliphates to the Persian Empires, the Chinese dynasties, and various states across South Asia—developed their own approaches to policing and social order.

In this chapter, we will examine some of these major Eastern empires. We will look at how religion, bureaucracy, cultural norms, and trade influenced policing structures. From the **muhtasib** in Islamic cities ensuring fair trade practices to the **yamen** offices in imperial China managing civil disputes, these systems offer a diverse view of how different societies approached the problem of maintaining security and justice.

1. Policing in the Early Islamic World

1.1. Emergence of the Caliphate and Sharia Law

With the rise of **Islam** in the 7th century CE, the Arabian Peninsula underwent rapid social and political transformations. After the Prophet Muhammad's death (632 CE), his successors (caliphs) established an Islamic Caliphate, expanding across the Middle East, North Africa, and parts of Asia and Europe.

Central to this new civilization was **Sharia**, the Islamic legal framework derived from the Quran, Hadith (traditions of the Prophet), and scholarly interpretations. Governance and policing were deeply tied to religious principles, emphasizing justice, fairness, and moral conduct.

1.2. The Role of the Muhtasib

A unique figure in many Islamic cities was the **muhtasib**. Often translated as a "market inspector" or "controller of public morals," the muhtasib had responsibilities that combined policing with market regulation.

- **Fair Trade:** The muhtasib ensured that merchants used honest weights and measures, preventing fraud. They could inspect shops, stalls, and warehouses, and fine or punish violators.
- **Morality and Public Conduct:** Beyond commerce, the muhtasib also enforced moral standards: no open public drinking of alcohol, no indecent behavior, and so forth.
- **Authority and Enforcement:** While not typically a uniformed "police officer" in the modern sense, the muhtasib had official backing. If someone refused to comply, the muhtasib could call upon guards or local officials to enforce rules.

This system reinforced the idea that economic life and moral order were inseparable under Islamic governance. The muhtasib, though local in focus, was part of a larger administrative hierarchy answering to the caliph or local emir (governor).

1.3. Military and Police Overlap

Similar to many empires, the Islamic Caliphate had **armies** that also performed internal security roles. Governors or military commanders could dispatch troops to quell rebellions, combat banditry, or enforce decrees in restive provinces. In large cities like Baghdad, Damascus, or Cairo, certain garrison units might be assigned to patrol gates and city streets, complementing the work of the muhtasib and local judges (qadis).

As the caliphate fractured into regional powers over the centuries—Umayyads, Abbasids, Fatimids, and later Ottoman rule—policing continued under various local rulers but retained many of these core features: a blend of religious principles, market regulation, and reliance on military forces when necessary.

2. The Persian Influence: From Sasanian to Safavid Eras

2.1. Sasanian Foundations

Prior to the Islamic conquests, Persia was ruled by the **Sasanian Empire** (224–651 CE). Renowned for its administrative sophistication, the Sasanians had officials who oversaw tax collection, religious affairs (Zoroastrian clergy), and local security. While details on specific policing roles are limited, historians note that the empire maintained a network of roads and couriers, allowing the central government to keep track of provincial governors.

2.2. Policing Under Islamic Persian Dynasties

After the Islamic conquest, Persian lands came under the caliphate, but later regained autonomy in various forms, such as the **Safavid Dynasty** (1501–1736). Safavid rulers combined Shi'a Islam with strong Persian administrative traditions:

- **Centralized Administration:** The shah (king) ruled from major cities like Isfahan, appointing governors to oversee provinces. These governors bore responsibility for law enforcement, gathering taxes, and managing local militias.
- **Urban Policing:** Large Persian cities had watchmen who patrolled bazaars (markets) and residential areas. They addressed theft, maintained order during festivals, and enforced local laws about modesty or religious behavior.
- **Religious Authorities:** As a Shi'a state, Safavid Persia had religious leaders with significant influence. They often worked alongside secular officials, ensuring that public morality aligned with state-endorsed religious norms.

In many respects, Persian policing mirrored the broader Islamic approach: a fusion of religious law, local watch systems, and strong central oversight by military forces when needed.

3. Imperial China: A Bureaucratic Approach to Law Enforcement

3.1. The Dynastic Cycle and Civil Administration

China's imperial history featured numerous dynasties—Han, Tang, Song, Yuan, Ming, and Qing—each building upon prior administrative legacies. A hallmark of imperial China was its vast **civil service system**, where scholars who passed rigorous exams could become officials. This bureaucracy influenced policing because local administration and justice were tightly interlinked.

3.2. The Yamen and Magistrates

At the local level, a **magistrate** presided over a **yamen**, which served as an administrative office and court. The magistrate was responsible for tax collection, judicial rulings, and local order. Supporting staff included constables, clerks, and bailiffs.

- **Constables (捕快, bǔkuài):** Tasked with arresting criminals, they often had local knowledge and networks of informants. They carried out magistrates' orders, delivering summons and apprehending suspects.
- **Maintaining Order:** The magistrate and his constables handled disputes, from land conflicts to theft. A portion of the yamen compound was used as a jail for pre-trial detention.
- **Influence of Confucianism:** Imperial China placed heavy emphasis on moral governance. Officials were expected to lead by example and maintain harmony through benevolent rule. Policing thus included a strong moral and educational component, discouraging wrongdoing through social pressure.

3.3. Punishments and Practices

Punishments in imperial China ranged from fines and forced labor to forms of corporal punishment (like caning) and, for severe crimes, the death penalty. The legal code spelled out detailed offenses and recommended penalties. Enforcement relied on confession-based evidence, although local officials did gather witness testimony and sometimes used rudimentary investigative methods.

3.4. Frontier Security and Military Garrisons

China's vast frontiers faced periodic invasions or raids from nomadic groups. To protect these borders, various dynasties built fortifications (such as the Great Wall) and stationed **military garrisons** in strategic locations. Soldiers in these outposts also served a policing function, controlling trade routes, checking travelers for permits, and suppressing banditry. In some regions, local ethnic groups were granted partial autonomy, with the imperial administration appointing overseers to ensure taxes and tributes were properly collected.

4. Policing Traditions in the Indian Subcontinent

4.1. Ancient and Medieval Roots

In the Indian subcontinent, policing practices date back to ancient times. The **Arthashastra**, an ancient Sanskrit treatise attributed to Kautilya (circa 4th century BCE), discussed governance, espionage, and methods of controlling crime. During the medieval era, various kingdoms—Chola, Gupta, and later the **Delhi Sultanate**—implemented versions of local watch systems and used military forces to maintain order.

4.2. The Mughal Empire

By the 16th century, much of the subcontinent fell under the **Mughal Empire**. Mughal rulers like Akbar, Jahangir, and Shah Jahan presided over a vast administration blending Persian-influenced structures with local Indian traditions:

- **Faujdars and Kotwals:** The **faujdars** were military commanders in charge of a district, responsible for general security. The **kotwal** was the head of a city's police, overseeing public order, market regulations, and cleanliness.
- **Market Supervision:** Like the muhtasib in Islamic cities, the kotwal ensured fair trade practices, regulated prices, and addressed corruption among traders.
- **Religious Diversity:** The Mughal Empire's population included Hindus, Muslims, Sikhs, Jains, and others. Policing had to accommodate varied customs. Akbar's policy of "Sulh-e-Kul" (universal peace) aimed for tolerance, though enforcement still leaned on the empire's Muslim identity.

4.3. Interplay of Local and Imperial Forces

In rural areas, local landowners (zamindars) often held authority over peasants, similar to feudal lords in Europe. They maintained private militias to enforce order on their estates and collect taxes. At the same time, imperial officials expected these zamindars to remain loyal and cooperate with Mughal governance. Conflict arose if a zamindar resisted imperial authority or misused power, triggering an imperial crackdown.

5. Southeast Asia, Japan, and Other Regions

5.1. Policing in Southeast Asian Kingdoms

Kingdoms in Southeast Asia (e.g., the Khmer Empire, Majapahit, Ayutthaya) developed their own patterns of policing influenced by Indian, Chinese, and local traditions. Rulers appointed officials who combined religious authority (often based on Hindu-Buddhist syncretism) with civil duties. In major cities, there were guard units to protect palaces, monitor markets, and enforce royal decrees. Local village chiefs handled minor disputes, following customary law.

5.2. Feudal Japan

In Japan, law enforcement was heavily shaped by **samurai** culture and the feudal system under the **shogunate**. Daimyō (feudal lords) controlled territories, with samurai serving as both warriors and local enforcers:

- **Samurai as Enforcers:** Samurai not only fought in wars but also enforced the social order in their domains. They had the right to use force if they perceived a challenge to their status.
- **Town Magistrates:** Larger cities like Edo (Tokyo), Osaka, and Kyoto had **machi-bugyō** (town magistrates) who oversaw policing, firefighting, and criminal investigations. They employed retainers known as **okappiki** to catch thieves and maintain street patrols.
- **Caste System:** Society was divided into samurai, peasants, artisans, and merchants. Policing often focused on keeping each class in its proper place, punishing peasants severely if they defied samurai authority.

While distinct in culture and structure, these Eastern traditions resemble Europe's pattern of local lords or officials controlling policing tasks within a larger imperial framework.

6. Trade Routes, Banditry, and the Spread of Policing Ideas

6.1. The Silk Road

Stretching from China through Central Asia to the Middle East and Europe, the **Silk Road** was a major conduit for commerce and cultural exchange. Securing these trade routes required cooperative policing across different empires. Caravans often hired armed guards. Cities along the route built walls and watchtowers. Local rulers sometimes negotiated safe passage treaties to encourage trade.

Banditry was a chronic problem. Empires recognized that if the Silk Road became too dangerous, merchants would avoid it, leading to economic losses. Hence, policing was both a local and international concern, as caravans crossed multiple political boundaries.

6.2. Maritime Trade

With the rise of maritime trade in the Indian Ocean, Southeast Asia, and East Asia, port cities thrived. Empires stationed **harbor masters** and **naval patrols** to collect customs dues, prevent smuggling, and protect merchant ships from pirates. Arabic, Chinese, Indian, and Southeast Asian vessels converged in bustling ports like Guangzhou, Malacca, Calicut, and Basra. Local rulers imposed policing structures to regulate these diverse trading communities, sometimes granting extraterritorial rights to foreign merchants, who would have their own "consular courts."

7. Religious Institutions and Law Enforcement

7.1. Islamic Courts and Qadis

In Islamic territories, **qadis** (judges) administered Sharia-based justice. They worked in tandem with local enforcers (like the muhtasib or governor's soldiers) to ensure that people followed Islamic law. Qadis heard civil and criminal cases, their verdicts enforced by local authorities. Large cities might have multiple qadis handling various districts.

7.2. Confucian Values in China

In imperial China, officials were often expected to embody Confucian virtues such as benevolence, righteousness, and propriety. Policing was therefore not just about punishing wrongdoing but also about guiding people to maintain social harmony. Education, moral suasion, and village mediations were seen as vital first steps, with formal punishment viewed as a last resort.

7.3. Hindu-Buddhist Traditions in Southeast Asia

In many Southeast Asian kingdoms, Hindu or Buddhist monasteries held social influence. Monks sometimes acted as mediators in local disputes, diminishing the need for violent or coercive law enforcement measures. Rulers, meanwhile, framed their authority in moral or religious terms, presenting themselves as protectors of dharma (righteousness). This moral underpinning shaped how policing was perceived and practiced.

8. Bureaucratic Efficiency and Its Limits

8.1. Record-Keeping and Administration

Eastern empires like China and certain Islamic caliphates maintained extensive bureaucracies, resulting in official records, census data, and judicial archives. These documents helped streamline governance. An official could theoretically trace a complaint or a criminal from one district to another, though corruption or local autonomy sometimes undermined the process.

8.2. Corruption and Regional Power

Despite detailed laws and administrative structures, corruption remained a persistent problem. Local governors, warlords, or influential families might subvert policing efforts for personal gain. In many parts of Asia, effective policing depended heavily on the caliber and morality of local officials. If an official was just and well-supported by the central government, law and order flourished. If not, policing broke down, and banditry or local feuds became rampant.

9. Comparing Eastern and Western Policing Traditions

Though we have primarily described these Eastern systems on their own terms, it is instructive to compare them with Western developments:

1. **Central vs. Local Control:** Both East and West had tension between centralized imperial or royal control and local autonomy. In the East, large empires like China or the Ottoman state had more sophisticated bureaucracies than many medieval European kingdoms.
2. **Religious Influence:** In Europe, the Church influenced moral and social policing. In the Islamic world, Sharia guided enforcement; in China, Confucian ideals; and in India, a mix of Hindu, Islamic, and local customs.
3. **Military-Policing Overlap:** Armies or elite guards often doubled as police in both East and West. From Roman legionnaires to Ottoman janissaries, from Chinese frontier troops to Japanese samurai, the line between soldier and policeman could blur.
4. **Market Regulation:** Whether the muhtasib, the Indian kotwal, or the European market bailiff, many societies recognized that trade and economic order demanded specialized policing.

Despite cultural differences, similar issues—tax collection, crime prevention, moral regulation, and controlling banditry—arose in every civilization.

10. Shifts in the Early Modern Period and Beyond

10.1. Gunpowder Empires

The Ottoman, Safavid, and Mughal states are sometimes referred to as the **Gunpowder Empires** due to their use of firearms in military expansion. As these empires stabilized vast territories, new administrative roles emerged, including specialized policing and intelligence units. For instance, the Ottomans had the **Janissaries**, who, while primarily a military corps, played internal security roles in major cities like Istanbul.

10.2. Foreign Interactions

European trade and colonization efforts in Asia—especially from the 16th century onwards—forced Eastern polities to adapt their policing. They needed to control foreign enclaves, oversee ports that received European ships, and handle new forms of crime related to global trade (like smuggling opium, as famously happened in China during the Qing Dynasty).

10.3. Evolution and Legacy

By the 18th and 19th centuries, many Eastern empires faced internal decline or external pressure, leading to reforms that introduced more "Western-style" policing in some areas. Yet the core traditions—local watchmen, combined religious and civic duties, and reliance on a strong central authority—remained influential in shaping these societies' conceptions of law enforcement.

Chapter 7

Transition to Early Modern Policing in Europe

In previous chapters, we traced the paths of policing in medieval Europe, rural communities, and across different Eastern Empires. We have seen how feudal lords, local officials, and religious institutions shared the responsibilities for law enforcement and social control. By the late medieval period (roughly the 14th and 15th centuries), key transformations were underway in Europe: the decline of feudalism, the rise of more powerful monarchies, the growth of trade and urban centers, and the spread of new ideas about governance. These changes set the stage for what historians often call the "early modern" era, spanning approximately the 15th to the 18th centuries (though exact dates vary by region).

This chapter focuses on how policing evolved during this early modern period in Europe. We will examine:

1. The gradual decline of purely feudal policing structures.
2. The rise of **absolute monarchies** in some regions and the emergence of more centralized forms of law enforcement.
3. The influence of **religious upheavals**, such as the Protestant Reformation and Catholic Counter-Reformation, on policing.
4. New forms of **city-based policing** and the early push for more consistent law enforcement in growing urban environments.
5. The beginnings of **state surveillance** and "secret police" techniques under monarchies eager to maintain power.
6. Shifts in the concept of justice and punishment influenced by early Enlightenment ideals (though fully formed Enlightenment thought would come later).

By the end of this chapter, we will see a Europe moving toward more standardized ways of enforcing laws, though the process was far from complete. Many medieval traditions endured, but the seeds of a more centralized and professional approach to policing were planted during this time.

1. Decline of Feudal Policing Models

1.1. Changing Roles of Lords and Vassals

In medieval Europe, feudal lords wielded significant power over local policing. They commanded private forces and held courts on their estates. However, from the 14th century onward, a series of events eroded feudal structures:

- **The Black Death** (mid-14th century) reduced populations and upended economies, undermining the rigid hierarchy between lords and peasants.
- **Growth of Cash Economies:** Instead of paying dues in labor or crops, peasants increasingly paid rents in money. This chipped away at the old obligations that had tied them to feudal lords.
- **Rise of Towns and Merchant Classes:** Wealthy merchants gained social and economic influence, making them less dependent on noble patronage.

These shifts weakened the direct policing authority of feudal nobles. They still had local armed men, but kings and central governments saw an opportunity to consolidate power and introduce their own representatives—officials like sheriffs or bailiffs—who reported directly to the crown. Over time, local lords found themselves under greater royal scrutiny, and their policing roles diminished relative to the increasing power of monarchs.

1.2. Centralizing Royal Power

Across Europe, the late medieval to early modern era saw monarchs who sought to unify laws, armies, and justice systems under their leadership. Examples include:

- The **Tudor Monarchs** in England (late 15th to early 17th century), who worked to reduce the influence of powerful nobles and build stronger institutions.
- The **Valois and Bourbon Dynasties** in France, which strove to create a centralized administration after periods of internal conflict.
- Similar patterns in Spain under the **Catholic Monarchs** (Ferdinand and Isabella) and later the Habsburgs, who reorganized governance in Iberia.

While these monarchs did not create modern police forces as we understand them, they laid groundwork by asserting that law enforcement was a royal prerogative. Sheriffs, constables, and other officers became increasingly accountable to the crown, not just local barons. In some cases, royal courts replaced feudal courts, bringing uniform laws and punishments across the kingdom.

2. The Emergence of Absolute Monarchies and Their Policing

2.1. Defining Absolutism

By the 17th century, in countries like France, the concept of **absolute monarchy** reached new heights. Absolutism, in theory, meant the monarch held all legislative and judicial power, unchallenged by nobles or assemblies. Rulers like Louis XIV of France famously declared, "I am the state," symbolizing near-total authority over governance.

2.2. Centralized Law Enforcement

Under absolute monarchies, controlling crime and dissent was crucial to maintaining the ruler's power. In France, for example:

- **Provost Marshals** and royal **baillis** enforced the king's justice in provinces.

- The crown appointed **lieutenant criminel** in some areas to oversee serious offenses, ensuring local courts aligned with the king's policies.
- Royal edicts standardized punishments and procedures. This did not replace local watchmen or constables but put them under a more formal royal framework.

Similar developments appeared in other absolutist states. In parts of Central Europe, rulers expanded their bureaucracies with officers responsible for policing roads, collecting tolls, and investigating crimes that could destabilize trade or incite rebellion. These were not uniformed police in the modern sense, but they represented an important step toward centralized control of law enforcement.

2.3. Secret Police and Spies

Absolute monarchies also feared conspiracies among nobles, foreign agents, or religious dissidents. As a result, some created informal or semi-formal **spy networks** to root out threats. While not always called "secret police," these agents performed surveillance tasks, reported suspicious activity, and sometimes orchestrated arrests on the monarch's behalf. In France, for example, Cardinal Richelieu under Louis XIII and later Cardinal Mazarin under Louis XIV employed spies and informers to maintain state security.

Though these systems were often ad hoc and varied from one monarchy to another, they signaled a growing idea: the state could keep close watch on its population, particularly on those who might undermine the ruler's authority. This idea would evolve further in later centuries, but its early roots appeared in the policing measures of absolute monarchs.

3. Religious Upheavals: The Reformation and Counter-Reformation

3.1. Policing Heresy and Religious Deviance

The Protestant Reformation, sparked by Martin Luther in 1517, and the subsequent Catholic Counter-Reformation changed Europe's religious landscape. Kings and princes aligned themselves with different confessions (Lutheran, Calvinist, Anglican, Catholic, etc.), turning religious belief into a matter of political loyalty.

Law enforcement adapted to this environment, as heresy and dissent were not merely spiritual offenses but threats to social harmony and royal authority. Princes or kings who embraced Protestantism policed Catholic practices, sometimes banning or seizing Catholic properties. Conversely, in Catholic regions, Protestant worshippers were persecuted. Secular officials—sheriffs, bailiffs, local militias—carried out the crackdown:

- **Investigations of Religion:** Officials might search homes for prohibited texts (such as Protestant Bibles in Catholic areas or vice versa).
- **Public Punishments:** Arrests and punishments for heresy served as a warning to others who might challenge the dominant faith.
- **Coordination with Church Authorities:** In many cases, bishops or religious courts guided the process, but secular law enforcement performed the actual arrests and detentions.

3.2. The Inquisition

In Catholic areas, the **Inquisition** worked closely with secular rulers to identify and punish heretics, especially after the Council of Trent (1545–1563) which intensified Counter-Reformation efforts. Although the Inquisition was an ecclesiastical institution, it often relied on state officials for manpower. Local constables or royal soldiers might detain suspects, turning them over to inquisitorial courts.

While the Inquisition is best known for its religious trials, the broader lesson is that religious conflicts shaped policing. Rulers realized that controlling religious dissent was just as important as controlling crime, as both could lead to social unrest. This tight link between religious and political authority contributed to the centralization of enforcement powers in the early modern period.

4. Urbanization and City-Based Policing

4.1. Expanding Towns and Markets

Between the 15th and 18th centuries, many European towns grew in size. Trade routes connected regions more effectively, and new financial centers emerged (Antwerp, Amsterdam, London, etc.). With more people living in close quarters, cities faced rising issues of theft, vagrancy, and disorder. Traditional watch-and-ward systems struggled to cope with larger populations.

4.2. City Guards and Night Watches

In response, towns hired **city guards** or **city watchmen**:

- **Paid Night Watch**: While earlier systems were often volunteer-based, some cities began paying watchmen, expecting them to patrol streets more regularly and remain vigilant.
- **Guild Participation**: Craftsmen's guilds sometimes helped fund or organize these guards, seeking to protect shops and merchandise in growing commercial areas.
- **Neighborhood Delegates**: In some places, each district or ward chose individuals to serve in the watch. This system could be more reliable than expecting the entire male population to take turns.

Cities also built or improved **city gates** and **walls**, controlling who entered or left after dark. Guards stationed at gates could question travelers, search for smuggled goods, and keep out known criminals. These measures show an increasing willingness by city authorities to assert control over urban environments, marking a step closer to professionalized policing.

4.3. Policing Public Morals

Urban policing also extended to moral regulations. City councils passed ordinances to maintain social discipline:

- **Curfews**: Some European cities enforced curfews for certain groups, such as apprentices, to prevent late-night rowdiness.
- **Regulating Taverns and Brothels**: Authorities tried to confine bawdy establishments to specific neighborhoods, hoping to reduce crime in central business districts.
- **Sumptuary Laws**: Similar to the medieval period, sumptuary laws governed what clothing people of various ranks could wear, though enforcement was often spotty.

While these efforts did not eliminate crime or vice, they established the principle that a municipal government had the right to regulate public behavior—a notion that would expand in later centuries.

5. Early Enlightenment Ideas and Their Impact

5.1. The Seeds of Legal Reform

Although the full Enlightenment movement belongs mostly to the 18th century, early voices in the 17th century (like Francis Bacon, René Descartes, and others) began questioning traditional authorities, urging systematic inquiry and rational governance. Over time, these ideas influenced some rulers to think about fairer laws and more reliable justice systems.

For instance, some monarchs or local councils:

- Simplified legal codes to make them more understandable.
- Introduced early measures to reduce torture or arbitrary imprisonment (though these changes were slow and uneven).
- Encouraged better record-keeping, so that officials could track criminals or suspects more systematically.

5.2. Philosophical Debates on Crime and Punishment

Toward the end of the early modern period, a few thinkers started to question the brutality of punishments that had long been accepted—public executions, mutilation, and torture. These criticisms did not necessarily result in immediate changes to policing, but they set the stage for future reforms. A desire for more humane treatment of criminals gradually took hold among segments of the educated elite, foreshadowing penal reforms in the late 18th and early 19th centuries.

6. The Evolving Roles of Local Officials

6.1. Sheriffs and Constables in Flux

As Europe moved into the 16th and 17th centuries, the offices of **sheriff** and **constable** persisted but adapted:

- **Sheriffs** in regions like England became more administrative, focusing on court duties, collecting fines, and overseeing prisons. In some countries, the title changed to reflect local languages or new administrative divisions.
- **Constables** in towns continued to handle day-to-day disorder. However, as cities expanded, some constables found it challenging to manage the volume of cases with minimal assistance or training.

In countries where absolute monarchies prevailed (such as France), local policing roles were overshadowed by royal appointees who wielded greater authority. Elsewhere, where power was more balanced between monarchs and regional estates (like parts of Germany or the Low Countries), local officials maintained greater autonomy.

6.2. The Justice of the Peace (JP)

In places like England, the **Justice of the Peace** (JP) became an influential figure. Officially recognized since the 14th century, JPs gained greater power in the 16th and 17th centuries:

- **Local Governance**: JPs handled minor cases in "petty sessions," relieving higher courts of routine matters.
- **Collaboration with Sheriffs and Constables**: They relied on constables to bring offenders before them.
- **Social Control**: JPs also enforced moral and social laws—ranging from vagrancy statutes to regulations on wages and prices.

This arrangement extended the reach of central government into rural life without requiring a vast, standing police force. JPs were typically local gentry who served without pay, motivated by status and a sense of duty.

7. Technology and Policing

7.1. Communications and Mobility

The early modern period saw improvements in road-building, the spread of the printing press, and the formation of postal networks. These developments, while modest compared to modern standards, improved communication for policing:

- **Postal Services**: Governments started using couriers more systematically to send warrants, official orders, or descriptions of wanted criminals.
- **Road Maintenance**: Better roads helped local officials travel for investigations or to deliver suspects to courts. Conversely, improved roads could also aid criminals' flight.

7.2. Firearms and Force

Firearms became more common, affecting how authorities handled rebellion or major disturbances. Armies and local militias trained with muskets, allowing them to suppress riots more effectively than medieval weaponry. However, the average constable or watchman still carried simpler arms (like clubs or swords). Widespread arming of local police was not common until much later.

8. Notable Regional Variations

8.1. The Italian City-States

During the Renaissance, Italian city-states (Venice, Florence, Milan, etc.) had complex administrative systems:

- **Guardie (Guards)**: Employed to patrol city streets, especially after dark.
- **Political Surveillance**: Rulers like the Medici in Florence used networks of informants to stay ahead of conspiracies.
- **Merchant Police**: Some trade guilds kept private security to protect valuable goods, especially in port cities like Genoa or Venice.

8.2. The Dutch Republic

In the Dutch Republic (16th–18th centuries), local magistrates called **schepenen** oversaw policing in towns. These merchant-driven urban centers valued stability for commerce, so they maintained well-organized civic guards. The Dutch also pioneered advanced financial institutions, and cities like Amsterdam put effort into curbing fraud, smuggling, and monetary crimes, using appointed officials to check markets and regulate banks.

8.3. Scandinavia

In regions such as Sweden or Denmark-Norway, kings gradually strengthened centralized rule, especially under leaders like Gustav Vasa in Sweden (16th century). Local **lensmenn** (bailiffs) oversaw rural districts, collecting taxes and maintaining order. Although the population remained relatively small, these countries also experienced an increase in written laws and codes that standardized punishments.

9. The Idea of "Police" Takes Shape in Language

9.1. Origin of the Word

Interestingly, the term "police" in English originates from the French "police," itself derived from the Greek "polis" (city). In the 17th and 18th centuries, "police" in French referred broadly to good order, governance, and public welfare. It was not yet used to mean a uniformed force; rather, it described the administration's role in regulating public life.

9.2. Publications on Policing

Writers in Germany and France produced treatises on "Polizeiwissenschaft" or "science of police," discussing how a ruler should organize society for health, safety, and moral order. These treatises covered topics like market regulation, fire safety, and controlling the spread of disease. While not strictly about catching criminals, they reflected a growing sense that the state had a responsibility to manage public welfare in a systematic way.

This conceptual shift—thinking of "police" as a broad function of governance—set the stage for more specialized and professional police forces in the 18th and 19th centuries. But during the early modern period, it mostly remained a theory of administrative oversight.

10. Toward Greater Uniformity in Punishments

10.1. Standardizing Laws and Penalties

As monarchs and councils gained more control, they worked to make laws and penalties more uniform. Codes like the **Carolina** in the Holy Roman Empire (issued under Emperor Charles V in 1532) and the **Ordonnance de Villers-Cotterêts** in France (1539) tried to standardize legal procedures, though local customs persisted. These codes clarified which crimes were punishable by death, which by imprisonment, and so on. They also outlined the roles of local officials in enforcing these penalties.

10.2. Public Executions and Their Significance

Public executions continued throughout the early modern era. Authorities believed dramatic spectacles deterred crime and demonstrated the state's power. People gathered in town squares to witness hangings, beheadings, or burnings at the stake. Though gruesome, these events reinforced the message that defying the law—whether religious, political, or criminal—had dire consequences. Over time, some intellectuals criticized such brutality, but the practice remained a mainstay of law enforcement until reforms in the late 18th century.

Chapter 8

Colonial Policing Models Around the World

The early modern period witnessed not only the centralization of policing in European states but also the dramatic expansion of European powers overseas. Starting in the 15th century with Portugal and Spain, and continuing into the 16th, 17th, and 18th centuries with the Dutch, British, French, and others, Europe's maritime empires spread across Africa, Asia, and the Americas. This colonial expansion included not just trade and settlement but also the imposition of law enforcement structures—often adapted from European forms like the sheriff-constable system or influenced by new challenges in unfamiliar territories.

In this chapter, we explore how Europeans enforced their will in colonies, how colonial authorities merged or conflicted with local policing traditions, and the impact of colonial rule on policing practices both in the colonies and back in Europe. We will address:

1. The earliest Spanish and Portuguese colonial policing strategies in the Americas.
2. The rise of Dutch and British colonial enclaves in Asia and Africa.
3. The adaptation of European legal and policing models to new societies with distinct cultures and governance.
4. How colonial militaries acted as primary enforcers, blending soldiering and policing.
5. The role of local collaborators or intermediaries in sustaining colonial order.
6. Early critiques and conflicts that arose from these imposed systems, foreshadowing later independence movements.

Through these examples, we see policing as a tool of empire: a means to secure commercial interests, maintain social hierarchies, and quell resistance. Although these systems varied across continents and centuries, they shared a core function: to uphold colonial authority through structured law enforcement.

1. Spanish and Portuguese Policing in the New World

1.1. Conquest and Encomienda

The Spanish conquest of the Americas began with Columbus in 1492, followed by conquistadors like Hernán Cortés in Mexico and Francisco Pizarro in Peru. The Portuguese, meanwhile, focused on Brazil after the Treaty of Tordesillas (1494). Once these powers established control over territories, they needed ways to maintain order and extract wealth, chiefly through systems like the **encomienda**, in which Spanish settlers were granted rights to native labor.

- **Military Enforcement:** Early on, conquest-era security was essentially military occupation. Conquistadors used armed force to deter rebellions, imposing their will on indigenous populations.
- **Colonial Officials:** Gradually, the Spanish Crown introduced officials such as **alcaldes** (magistrates) and **corregidores** (local governors) to administer towns. These individuals combined judicial, administrative, and policing powers.
- **Native Auxiliaries:** Some indigenous leaders cooperated with conquerors, providing local enforcers who knew the land and people. However, this collaboration often created tension within native communities.

1.2. Laws of the Indies and Judicial Framework

The Spanish Crown issued the **Laws of the Indies**—a body of regulations intended to govern colonial life, including the treatment of indigenous peoples. In theory, these laws protected natives from extreme abuses, but in practice, enforcement was uneven. Officials in distant regions had considerable leeway, and corruption could be rampant. Policing in frontier areas was often more about securing economic interests—silver mines in Peru or Mexico, for instance—than ensuring justice for all subjects.

1.3. Portuguese Brazil

In Brazil, Portuguese captaincies were distributed to noble supporters, similar to feudal grants. These **donatários** acted as governors, organizing their own militias and local officials to maintain order. As sugar plantations expanded, African slaves replaced or supplemented indigenous labor. Over time, controlling enslaved populations became a key policing function in Portuguese colonies, as it did in other slave-based economies.

2. French, Dutch, and English Colonial Policing Approaches

2.1. Dutch in Asia: The VOC

The **Dutch East India Company** (VOC) wielded quasi-governmental powers in parts of Asia, especially in the Indonesian archipelago. It hired soldiers and built forts, using a mix of diplomacy, trade agreements, and force to control local populations. Policing tasks—protecting warehouses, ships, and trade routes—were handled by VOC employees who could arrest or punish suspected thieves or smugglers.

- **Local Alliances:** The Dutch often used existing rulers (sultans or regional kings) as intermediaries. They granted these leaders some autonomy in local affairs, but insisted on exclusive trade rights.
- **Fortified Bases:** In major outposts like Batavia (now Jakarta), the VOC established councils that combined judicial, administrative, and policing powers. Dutch authorities occasionally clashed with local traditions, imposing European practices that sometimes provoked resistance.

2.2. French Expeditions and Settlements

France established colonies in the Caribbean, North America (New France in Canada, Louisiana), and parts of Africa and Asia in later centuries. As with other colonial powers:

- **Military Garrisons:** Initially, soldier-settlers were responsible for policing. Commanders managed the day-to-day discipline of small settler communities.
- **Intendants and Governors:** Over time, France sent royal officials—called **intendants**—to oversee finance and justice, including policing matters. They worked with local militias or newly formed colonial constables to handle routine crime.
- **Native Partnerships:** In some regions, French explorers allied with indigenous groups against rival tribes or European competitors. French officers might rely on local warriors for policing tasks, especially in remote fur-trading territories.

2.3. British Colonies in North America

The English, later British, colonization of North America introduced **sheriff-constable** models in the Thirteen Colonies, reflecting English tradition. Towns in New England often had local watch systems, while in southern colonies, **slave patrols** emerged as a distinct form of policing:

- **County Sheriffs:** In the southern colonies, the county sheriff was often the main law enforcer, collecting taxes, serving court orders, and pursuing felons.
- **Night Watches:** Towns like Boston, New York, and Philadelphia developed night watches to address petty crime and fire threats. As populations grew, so did demands for more organized policing.
- **Slave Patrols:** In slaveholding regions, patrols existed to prevent revolts and catch runaway slaves. They combined features of militias and law enforcement, demonstrating how policing was intertwined with social and economic structures—especially racial hierarchy.

3. The Role of Colonial Militaries as Police Forces

3.1. Overlapping Functions

In many colonies, there was no clear line between soldier and policeman. Colonial armies or garrisons primarily defended territory from rival powers or indigenous uprisings. But in day-to-day life, they also enforced laws, collected taxes, and protected trade. This overlap was especially visible on frontiers, where a fort or station housed the only official representatives of the colonial government.

3.2. Suppression of Revolts and Riots

Colonial authorities dealt with frequent rebellions or uprisings—indigenous groups resisting conquest, enslaved persons revolting on plantations, or settlers protesting tax policies. Soldiers suppressed these revolts:

- **Use of Force:** Lethal methods were employed to crush rebellions swiftly. Punitive expeditions burned villages or fields to deter further resistance.
- **Martial Law:** In emergencies, governors declared martial law, allowing military officers to arrest civilians and impose severe punishments without lengthy trials.
- **Long-Term Consequences:** Heavy-handed tactics fueled resentment and set precedents for future conflicts, shaping the colonies' political landscape well into later centuries.

4. Local Collaborators and Intermediaries

4.1. Indirect Rule in Africa and Asia

Some colonial powers, particularly the British in parts of Africa and Asia, used a system often called **"indirect rule."** Instead of replacing local governance structures outright, they co-opted existing chiefs, sultans, or princes, expecting these local figures to enforce colonial laws and collect taxes in exchange for autonomy or material benefits.

- **Advantages for the Colonial Power:** Fewer resources spent on direct administration or policing, as local rulers handled day-to-day enforcement.

- **Issues of Legitimacy:** Local elites who cooperated with colonizers sometimes lost legitimacy with their people, seen as "puppets" of foreign rulers.
- **Hybrid Policing Methods:** Traditional policing customs (like clan-based conflict resolution) merged with European-style courts and procedures, leading to complex legal and enforcement systems.

4.2. Creole and Mestizo Populations

In Latin America, a class of **criollos** (people of Spanish descent born in the colonies) gained social and economic power over time, often filling administrative or policing roles. In Brazil and other regions, individuals of mixed heritage (mestiços, mulattos, etc.) sometimes served as intermediaries, bridging colonial and indigenous or African communities. Policing in these contexts reinforced social hierarchies based on race and status.

5. Plantation Societies and Slave Codes

5.1. Policing Enslaved Populations

Wherever plantation economies flourished—such as the Caribbean, southern American colonies, or parts of Brazil—law enforcement centered on maintaining control over enslaved labor:

- **Slave Codes:** These were sets of laws restricting the movement, assembly, and behavior of enslaved people. They prescribed harsh punishments for infractions and gave wide authority to slave owners and patrols.
- **Runaway Hunts:** Local militias or professional slave catchers tracked down fugitives. Rewards were offered for returning escaped enslaved persons.
- **Fear Tactics:** Public whippings and executions were used to dissuade rebellion, mirroring the spectacle punishments seen in Europe but with a strong racial component.

5.2. Impact on Policing Culture

These brutal systems shaped how policing was perceived in plantation societies. Law enforcement became deeply connected to the defense of property rights in human beings, reinforcing an authoritarian style. Even after slavery's eventual abolition in various parts of the world, the legacies of these control tactics persisted, influencing post-colonial policing models.

6. Exporting the Sheriff-Constable Model and Other European Practices

6.1. Adaptation in North American Colonies

As mentioned, British colonies in North America transplanted the **sheriff-constable** system. Local assemblies passed statutes defining these officers' duties, often mirroring English law. Meanwhile, the night watch tradition also came from England but evolved to suit colonial cities' demographics and layouts. Over time, these structures formed the backbone of American law enforcement well into the 18th and early 19th centuries.

6.2. French and Spanish Legacies

In Canada (New France) and Louisiana, French practices took root, while Spanish governance shaped policing in territories like Florida, Texas, and California. Even after these areas came under British or American control, traces of Spanish or French legal concepts lingered in property laws, civil codes, and local policing traditions.

6.3. Dutch Legal Influence

In places like South Africa (initially settled by the Dutch), laws derived from **Roman-Dutch law** formed the basis of policing and justice systems. When the British took over the Cape Colony in the early 19th century, they layered their own statutes on top, creating a hybrid system that combined Dutch legal traditions with British-style policing offices.

7. Early Conflicts and Resistance

7.1. Pirate Havens and Smuggling

Policing the high seas became important for colonial powers, as piracy threatened shipping routes. Some pirates found refuge in coastal towns willing to ignore their activities for a share of profits. European navies and colonial officials tried to clamp down, establishing maritime patrols. Smuggling of goods—especially around strict monopolies on tobacco or sugar—likewise challenged colonial authorities, forcing them to develop more sophisticated methods of monitoring ports and coastlines.

7.2. Indigenous Resistance

Indigenous peoples worldwide contested colonial encroachment:

- **Armed Rebellions:** Some fought back in organized wars, like the Pueblo Revolt in what is now the southwestern United States, or the Mapuche resistance in Chile.
- **Local Policing Traditions:** Pre-colonial societies often had their own systems of conflict resolution and community defense. Colonizers typically overlooked these traditions, imposing foreign laws that clashed with indigenous customs.
- **Negotiated Autonomy:** In some instances, European officials gave partial recognition to traditional chiefs, expecting them to maintain order according to colonial frameworks. This mixed approach could cause internal conflicts as indigenous communities debated whether to collaborate or resist.

7.3. Slave Revolts and Maroon Communities

Enslaved Africans also resisted colonial policing by escaping to remote regions. **Maroon communities** formed in places like Jamaica, Suriname, and Brazil, establishing independent societies outside colonial control. Authorities treated these communities as threats, dispatching militias or special expeditions to recapture them. Ongoing conflicts highlighted the limited reach of colonial policing in challenging terrains.

8. Influence of Colonial Experiences on European Policing

8.1. Administrators Returning Home

Colonial administrators often returned to Europe after years in service. Their experiences shaped ideas about discipline, law enforcement, and the use of force:

- **Printed Manuals and Reports:** Some wrote treatises or guides on how to manage native populations or suppress rebellions. Although these were colonial in focus, they sometimes influenced debates on metropolitan policing back in Europe.
- **Military-Style Policing at Home:** The notion of using well-trained, centralized forces to control civilian populations, tested in colonies, informed future reforms. Rulers or councils might see the benefits of organized, disciplined policing in European cities as well.

8.2. Transfer of Personnel and Methods

Armies and navies circulated between colonial and European stations. Officers who had served in colonial contexts occasionally applied the same tactics upon returning to the continent—especially for riot control or addressing slums. While 18th-century Europe was not wholly militarized, there was a gradual acceptance that state power could be projected more intensively to maintain order, reflecting lessons learned abroad.

9. Critiques and Consequences

9.1. Early Criticisms of Colonial Policing

Not all Europeans approved of the harsh methods used in colonies. Missionaries, traders with humanitarian leanings, or Enlightenment-influenced thinkers sometimes reported abuses—massacres, torture, or excessive crackdowns—raising moral and philosophical questions:

- **Religious Appeals:** Clergy might condemn brutalities against indigenous or enslaved peoples, urging more compassionate approaches.
- **Philosophical Arguments:** Writers influenced by the ideals of liberty and natural rights occasionally denounced the hypocrisy of oppressive colonial policing.
- **Economic Considerations:** Some argued that less coercive systems would be more profitable in the long run, as they would foster cooperation from local populations.

Although these critiques rarely halted colonial expansion, they contributed to evolving debates about governance, justice, and the limits of state power.

9.2. Seeds of Future Nationalism

Colonial policing often sowed the seeds of **nationalist** or **independence** movements. As local elites or educated classes came into contact with Enlightenment ideas about rights and sovereignty, they questioned foreign domination and the policing structures that upheld it. Over time, these sentiments would pave the way for rebellions and revolutions in the 18th, 19th, and 20th centuries, although that goes beyond our current historical scope.

Chapter 9

Police under Absolute Monarchies

In Chapter 7, we observed how early modern European monarchies expanded their powers over law enforcement, gradually centralizing many policing functions. In Chapter 8, we turned to colonial policing models, where European states imposed their administrative and military might on distant lands. Now, in Chapter 9, we delve more specifically into the phenomenon of **absolute monarchies**—systems in which rulers claimed nearly unchallenged authority over their realms.

While not all early modern and pre-modern kings and queens wielded absolute power, certain states epitomized the idea. France under Louis XIV (reigned 1643–1715) is the classic example, but smaller states in central Europe, as well as Russia under the Tsars, also pushed toward autocratic control during the 17th and 18th centuries. In many of these cases, law enforcement became an arm of the monarch's centralized administration, ensuring the ruler's edicts were followed and suppressing any sign of dissent.

In this chapter, we will examine:

1. The defining features of absolute monarchy and how these shaped policing structures.
2. The bureaucratic and administrative apparatus that supported royal power and extended into the realm of local and regional policing.
3. The rise of special security agencies, often referred to as "secret police," responsible for monitoring suspected rebels or conspirators.
4. Practical methods used by monarchs to enforce social order, including censorship, surveillance, and swift punishments.
5. Variations among different absolute regimes, such as Bourbon France, Habsburg Austria, Prussia under the Hohenzollerns, and Tsarist Russia.
6. Critiques and limitations of these methods, including corruption, local resistance, and the seeds of future revolutions that would challenge absolute power.

By the end of this chapter, we will see that while absolute monarchies advanced a more unified and centralized notion of "police," they also sowed dissatisfaction among their subjects. These policing methods—sometimes harsh and intrusive—sparked debates about rights, freedoms, and the legitimacy of unchecked royal authority, laying the groundwork for Enlightenment critiques that we will explore in Chapter 10.

1. Defining Absolutism and Its Impact on Policing

1.1. Absolutism as a Political Theory

Absolutism refers to a form of monarchy where the ruler claims complete authority within the state—above feudal lords, church leaders, or parliaments. In theory, an absolutist monarch stands as the sole fountain of law, making edicts that apply uniformly across the realm. This concept, famously encapsulated by Louis XIV's (apocryphal) statement, "L'État, c'est moi" ("I am the state"), found expression in various regions of Europe during the 17th and 18th centuries.

1.2. Centralizing Law Enforcement

For monarchs to implement absolute rule, they needed reliable mechanisms of control. Policing thus became vital. No longer could the king rely solely on local nobles or fragmented feudal systems. Instead, the crown worked to create:

- **Royal Intendants or Governors**: Officials appointed directly by the monarch to oversee provinces and ensure local compliance with royal directives. These officials often had policing authority, commanding local militias or watch units.

- **Uniform Legal Codes**: Attempts were made to standardize laws and procedures, reducing the patchwork of local customs. Codification allowed the monarch to centralize punishment for crimes and set uniform standards for policing.
- **Professionalized Officials**: While still a far cry from a "modern" civil service, many absolutist regimes introduced some level of training or guidelines for local enforcers, ensuring loyalty to the throne.

2. The Administrative Framework of Absolute Monarchies

2.1. Royal Councils and Ministries

Absolute monarchs typically governed through councils or ministries that dealt with different aspects of the state—finance, war, foreign affairs, and justice. A minister or secretary responsible for "police," "internal affairs," or "public order" might emerge over time. This shift away from purely feudal or ad hoc structures meant that policing was no longer a loose patchwork but an element of the king's broader administrative system.

- **Ministry of Police (France)**: In 17th- and 18th-century France, the monarchy developed offices specifically concerned with internal security. Over time, this bureaucracy evolved, culminating in more structured organizations by the time of the French Revolution (though that is beyond our current scope).
- **Russian Colleges**: Under Peter the Great (r. 1682–1725), Russia reorganized its government into "colleges," each overseeing a specific function, from war to justice. Policing duties fell under certain colleges responsible for internal order, with local voivodes (provincial governors) and gentry officers carrying out decrees.

2.2. Provincial and Local Officials

Below the central administration were **intendants** (in France), **governors**, or **commissioners** who enforced royal authority in the provinces. These officials had the power to:

- Raise local militias or call upon military detachments for significant disturbances.

- Oversee city guards or watchmen.
- Investigate crimes, especially if they threatened the king's interests or the stability of the realm.

They often faced resistance from local elites who preferred traditional, decentralized ways of policing. Nonetheless, the monarchy's administrative power usually prevailed, particularly in states where the nobility had been subdued or co-opted.

2.3. Funding and Sustaining Centralized Policing

Absolute rulers needed to pay for these administrative and policing structures. Mercantilist economic policies, taxation reforms, and increased trade revenues helped fund larger bureaucracies. The state's ability to raise taxes was crucial: without consistent revenue, the monarchy could not maintain a standing army or a network of loyal officials to enforce laws.

3. Secret Police and Surveillance

3.1. Emergence of Covert Agencies

One hallmark of many absolute monarchies was the reliance on **secret police** or espionage networks to root out dissent. Although these agencies varied widely across different states, their functions typically included:

- **Monitoring Nobles**: Even after many nobles were integrated into the monarchy's system (through titles, court appointments, etc.), they could still pose a threat if they conspired. Secret informers reported on noble gatherings or suspect communications.
- **Suppressing Political Plots**: Potential rebellions, conspiracies, or unauthorized assemblies were investigated. Suspects might be detained without public trials, reflecting the monarch's unchecked power.
- **Censorship**: Control over printing presses and the dissemination of written materials was also a form of policing. Authorities seized seditious pamphlets or books.

3.2. Famous Examples: France and Russia

- **France**: Cardinals Richelieu and Mazarin (under Louis XIII and Louis XIV) nurtured extensive spy networks. Later, under Louis XV, the "Secret du Roi" served as a private intelligence service answering directly to the king, bypassing official channels.
- **Russia**: Tsarist regimes utilized the **Oprichnina** under Ivan the Terrible in the 16th century (an earlier form of terror-policing), and by the 18th century, Tsars like Catherine the Great maintained a strong tradition of informers and secret tribunals, though these were not always called "police" in a formal sense.

3.3. Impact on Daily Life

While these secret police functions mainly targeted political threats, they also influenced everyday life for subjects of an absolute monarch. Public speech could be curtailed if it criticized the king or his policies. People learned to watch what they said, aware that informers might be present. This climate of fear was both a strength and a weakness for absolute states: it could deter rebellion in the short term but also bred resentment.

4. Practical Methods of Enforcement

4.1. Routinely Harsh Punishments

Absolute monarchies often enforced severe punishments to deter crime and political defiance:

- **Public Executions and Torture**: Traditional methods of punishment persisted, including beheadings, hangings, drawing and quartering, and torture to extract confessions. The monarchy used these as public spectacles of power.
- **Imprisonment in State Facilities**: Some states built or expanded prisons or fortress-like facilities (e.g., the Bastille in France) where political prisoners could be held indefinitely on the king's orders.
- **Forced Labor**: Offenders might be sent to galleys (in maritime states), forced to row on naval ships for years, or assigned to large-scale building projects.

4.2. Controls on Movement and Identity

Absolute monarchies sometimes introduced early forms of **internal passports** or required travel documents to move between provinces. This gave authorities a means to track suspicious persons. Innkeepers might be ordered to report strangers staying overnight, and local watchmen could demand proof of identity. Although not universal, these measures represented a growing effort by the state to monitor the population's movements.

4.3. Policing Morality and Social Norms

Beyond politics and crime, many absolute rulers claimed moral authority as part of their right to govern. They might enforce:

- **Religion**: In Catholic states, authorities could police religious conformity in tandem with church officials, penalizing Protestants or other minorities. In Protestant monarchies, Catholicism or other practices might be restricted.
- **Sumptuary Laws and Public Decency**: Some states regulated clothing, festivals, and personal conduct, much like earlier periods, but now with the crown's backing.
- **Guild Regulations and Market Controls**: Monarchs who followed mercantilist policies might direct local officials to regulate trade strictly, punishing unauthorized sales or smuggling.

5. Regional Variations in Absolute Monarchies

5.1. France under the Bourbons

The French monarchy provides the quintessential example of absolutism, especially under Louis XIV. He weakened the power of noble families by luring them to the lavish court at Versailles, where they were kept occupied with court ritual and etiquette. Meanwhile, he sent **intendants** to the provinces, giving them policing and administrative authority to ensure that tax collection ran smoothly and that local officials followed the royal line. A network of spies and informers kept watch for sedition.

5.2. Prussia under the Hohenzollerns

In Prussia, a smaller but emerging power in the 17th and 18th centuries, the Hohenzollern rulers developed a strong military culture. The monarchy's emphasis on discipline and order extended to policing:

- **Garrison Towns**: Many Prussian towns had large garrisons. Soldiers often acted as local enforcers, stepping in to quell riots or arrest criminals.
- **State Bureaucracy**: Prussia became known for its efficient bureaucracy, with officials trained to enforce royal decrees. This system would later influence policing models in German states into the 19th century.

5.3. Austria and the Habsburg Lands

The sprawling Habsburg realms (Austria, Bohemia, parts of Hungary) were diverse in language, religion, and culture. Centralization was challenging, but rulers like Maria Theresa (r. 1740–1780) and Joseph II (r. 1780–1790) pushed administrative reforms. Policing in these lands often combined local traditions with new, more uniform codes. Imperial officials strove to bring distant provinces under tighter control, deploying soldiers and officials to enforce the Habsburg agenda.

5.4. Russian Tsardom

Russia's path to absolutism was unique. After centuries of Mongol rule, the Tsars centralized authority in Moscow. Ivan the Terrible used terror to break boyar (noble) power, employing the infamous Oprichnina. By the 18th century, Peter the Great and Catherine the Great accelerated Western-inspired reforms, building a bureaucracy, expanding the army, and imposing their will on vast territories. They faced ongoing challenges policing large, rural expanses with limited infrastructure. Still, the Tsar's word was theoretically absolute; local officials, drawn from the nobility, enforced these decrees via a combination of force and patronage.

6. Challenges and Critiques

6.1. Corruption and Inefficiency

Despite the grandeur of absolute monarchies, corruption could cripple their policing systems:

- **Bribery**: Officials, especially in remote areas, might accept bribes to look the other way.
- **Nepotism**: Powerful families placed relatives in positions of authority, prioritizing loyalty over competence.
- **Slow Communication**: Even with improved roads, it could take days or weeks for orders to travel from the capital to distant provinces, limiting the crown's ability to act swiftly.

Over time, these inefficiencies tarnished the monarchy's reputation for delivering justice, feeding dissent among commoners and middle-class citizens who wanted more predictability and fairness.

6.2. Noble Resistance

Some nobility accepted roles in the king's administration, but others resisted. They might continue to police their estates as they saw fit, ignoring or bending royal edicts. If a noble felt pushed too far, they could conspire with like-minded peers. Although large-scale noble revolts were less common by the 18th century (compared to earlier eras), the threat persisted, prompting monarchs to maintain vigilance through their secret police.

6.3. Public Discontent and Enlightenment Ideas

By the late 17th and 18th centuries, new currents of thought questioned the legitimacy of absolute monarchies. Philosophers argued about the "social contract" and natural rights, implying that the monarch's power should have limits. Harsh or arbitrary policing—public punishments, secret arrests—could stir outrage, particularly among educated elites who read Enlightenment literature. Though these critiques would come to a head in the Age of Revolutions (late 18th century onward), the seeds were already there.

7. Punishment, Spectacle, and Attempts at Reform

7.1. Judicial Reforms

Some absolute monarchs recognized that an overly brutal legal system could undermine their own goals. A few introduced limited reforms:

- **Restrictions on Torture**: Figures like Frederick the Great of Prussia publicly disapproved of torture, limiting its use in trials.
- **Simplifying Legal Codes**: Rulers such as Maria Theresa and Joseph II in the Habsburg Empire sought to unify and clarify laws, aiming to reduce arbitrary rulings.
- **Codification**: The Russian Tsars periodically attempted new legal codes (like the Ulozhenie under Tsar Alexei in 1649) to systematize criminal and civil law.

Though far from modern liberal standards, these changes indicated some rulers' desire for a more orderly, less chaotic enforcement system.

7.2. The Persistence of Public Punishments

Despite incremental reforms, spectacle punishments endured. Public hangings, floggings, and pillory events kept the population reminded of the monarchy's power. Prisons were generally grim, used mainly for those awaiting trial or political detainees. Long-term incarceration as a primary punishment was still relatively uncommon; quick, harsh penalties were deemed more effective at deterring wrongdoing.

7.3. Social Control Measures

Absolute monarchies also believed in policing as a method of "improving" society:

- **Poor Relief and Vagrancy Laws**: Rulers saw idle populations as potential sources of disorder. They might forcibly employ vagrants or require them to move to designated areas.
- **Family and Marriage Regulations**: Some states regulated marriage licenses, concerned that illegitimate births or unwed couples would lead to poverty and crime.
- **Urban Planning**: In capital cities, monarchs sometimes invested in street lighting, improved roads, or set up "city guard" forces to show their benevolence and keep order.

8. Influence on Neighboring States

8.1. Imitation of French Institutions

France under Louis XIV was widely admired or feared for its administrative might. Courts across Europe tried to replicate aspects of French bureaucracy and policing. They sent envoys to study French institutions or hired French administrators. This led to a cross-pollination of policing ideas. However, local traditions and power structures meant no two states were exactly alike.

8.2. Wars and Alliances

Absolute monarchs also fought frequent wars, forming and dissolving alliances. After each conflict, newly acquired territories had to be policed, requiring expansions of garrisons and local administrators. Occupation forces sometimes found themselves acting as a police presence in unfamiliar lands, clashing with locals who resented foreign rule.

9. The Seeds of Change

9.1. Enlightenment Critiques

A growing body of Enlightenment thinkers—John Locke (in an earlier period), Montesquieu, Voltaire, and Rousseau, among others—challenged the foundations of absolute rule. While not all directly addressed "policing," their broader arguments about individual rights, the separation of powers, and the social contract implicitly criticized arbitrary law enforcement. If sovereignty truly rested with "the people," then the monarch's right to spy, torture, or indefinitely imprison citizens came into question.

9.2. Economic and Social Shifts

By the 18th century, commercial and industrial developments began to alter Europe's social fabric. A new middle class (the bourgeoisie) emerged, invested in trade, manufacturing, and finance. These citizens demanded stability and fairness in the legal system, not just the caprices of an autocratic ruler. Their economic power gave them leverage to push for reforms, including more consistent policing.

9.3. Pre-Revolutionary Tensions

Towards the late 18th century, states like France, Russia, and parts of Central Europe experienced financial crises and social unrest. Heavy taxation, economic inequality, and resentment of noble privileges contributed to a volatile environment. Absolute monarchies, with their top-down policing structures, struggled to handle broad-based discontent without resorting to brutal repression. This environment would soon spark major upheavals—most notably, the French Revolution of 1789—reshaping the course of policing and governance worldwide.

Chapter 10

Enlightenment Ideals and Policing

In Chapter 9, we examined how absolute monarchies used centralized, often harsh policing to maintain power. We concluded by noting that, over time, new ideas—commonly grouped under the banner of the **Enlightenment**—challenged the foundations of absolute authority. This chapter focuses on how those Enlightenment ideals gradually influenced policing concepts, laws, and practices in the 18th century and into the early 19th century.

The Enlightenment was characterized by a confidence in human reason, skepticism toward tradition, and a strong interest in improving society through rational governance. Philosophers questioned traditional justifications for autocratic rule, aristocratic privilege, and brutal punishments. They proposed that a fair and consistent legal system, designed to preserve the natural rights of citizens, would promote both security and moral development.

Here, we will explore:

1. Key Enlightenment thinkers and their contributions to ideas about law and punishment.
2. The rise of **humanitarian** and **rational** perspectives on crime, focusing on deterrence and rehabilitation rather than pure retribution.
3. Changes in legal codes and procedures that reflected these new ideals, including a gradual move away from torture and arbitrary imprisonment.
4. The creation of institutions and methods of policing that emphasized a more systematic, predictable approach.
5. How these shifts intersected with political upheavals, especially the American and French Revolutions (though we will not delve into detailed modern developments), which further tested and spread Enlightenment-based policing ideas.

By examining these Enlightenment transformations, we see the seeds of the modern notion of "police" as a public service—an entity that exists not just to enforce a ruler's will, but also to uphold social order for the benefit of citizens, ideally under transparent and reasonable laws.

1. Philosophical Foundations

1.1. Reason, Liberty, and the Social Contract

Central to Enlightenment thought was the idea that legitimate political authority stems from a social contract—a conceptual agreement among individuals to form a society for mutual benefit. Philosophers such as **Thomas Hobbes**, **John Locke**, and later **Jean-Jacques Rousseau** shaped these discussions:

- **Locke** argued that individuals possess natural rights (life, liberty, property). Government exists primarily to protect these rights, and policing should serve the public rather than oppress it.
- **Rousseau** emphasized the "general will," suggesting that laws should reflect the collective interest, not the whims of an autocrat. This notion opened the door to more democratic oversight of policing functions.

1.2. Montesquieu and the Separation of Powers

In his work *The Spirit of the Laws* (1748), **Montesquieu** proposed separating government powers into executive, legislative, and judicial branches to prevent tyranny. This had implications for policing, which was traditionally controlled by monarchs or local lords. If policing aligned with an independent judiciary, it could act more impartially, reducing arbitrary arrests or punishments. While full realization of this separation took many more decades, Montesquieu's ideas laid theoretical groundwork.

1.3. Voltaire's Critique of Injustice

Voltaire used satire and reasoned argument to criticize unfair trials and excessive punishments. He championed the cause of wrongly convicted individuals (e.g., the Calas case in France) to show the dangers of a system lacking due process. Voltaire's emphasis on tolerance and justice resonated with emerging calls to reform policing practices that relied on torture, forced confessions, or indefinite detention.

2. Cesare Beccaria and Penal Reform

2.1. *On Crimes and Punishments* (1764)

One of the most direct and influential Enlightenment works on policing and criminal justice was **Cesare Beccaria's** *Dei delitti e delle pene* (*On Crimes and Punishments*), published in 1764. Beccaria, an Italian philosopher and jurist, argued that laws and punishments should be:

- **Proportional** to the crime.
- Designed to deter, not inflict gratuitous cruelty.
- Public, prompt, and consistent, so people clearly understand the consequences of wrongdoing.

Beccaria's call to end torture and the death penalty for most offenses marked a drastic departure from prevailing norms. He believed severe punishments often failed to prevent crime and could erode the moral fabric of society.

2.2. Influence on Policy

Beccaria's treatise spread widely, translated into several languages. Monarchs like **Catherine the Great** of Russia and reform-minded rulers in central Europe showed interest in his ideas, though practical application varied. Enlightened monarchs selectively adopted reforms that improved their image without fully surrendering autocratic power.

In Western Europe, thinkers and legal reformers increasingly cited Beccaria when pushing to limit torture, standardize procedures, and reduce the range of capital offenses. Although the pace of change was uneven, the direction was clear: a more rational, humanitarian view of crime and punishment was taking root.

3. Humanitarian Trends in Criminal Law

3.1. Decline of Torture

Under Enlightenment pressure, several states began to limit or abolish torture as a means of interrogation:

- **Prussia**: Frederick the Great banned judicial torture in most cases.
- **Austria**: Maria Theresa and later Joseph II moved toward more lenient practices, though they did not always implement them universally.
- **France**: Public opinion turned against judicial torture, and while the monarchy was slow to fully ban it, usage declined in practice.

3.2. Reduced Reliance on Capital Punishment

Beccaria and other reformers argued that certainty of punishment mattered more than severity. Some countries restricted capital punishment to the most serious crimes, introducing imprisonment or forced labor for others. While public executions did not disappear overnight, the range of offenses punishable by death started to shrink in many parts of Europe.

3.3. Rise of Penitentiaries (in Concept)

Although the widespread establishment of modern prisons belongs more to the 19th century, Enlightenment ideas laid the intellectual groundwork. Reformers began to consider **incarceration** not just as a holding method pre-trial, but as a potential punishment in itself—one that might rehabilitate the offender. Debates about prison design and discipline, as well as moral instruction, emerged in Enlightenment circles, foreshadowing developments in the decades to come.

4. Shifts in Policing Philosophy and Practice

4.1. Policing as Public Service

Prior to the Enlightenment, policing largely served the ruling class or monarchy. Enlightenment thinkers introduced the notion that policing should protect **all** members of society, ensuring safety and justice for the common good. This ideal, while not fully realized, influenced local reforms:

- **Community Involvement**: Some towns experimented with more structured "night watch" or "patrol" systems, funded by municipal budgets rather than private patrons.
- **Regulation vs. Rights**: Enlightenment-inspired officials grappled with balancing the state's regulatory interest (health, safety, morality) against individual freedoms.

4.2. Early Statistics and Record-Keeping

A growing scientific mindset encouraged data collection, including crime statistics and population records. Enlightenment officials in places like Austria, Prussia, and certain Italian states tried to gather more precise information about criminal occurrences:

- **Tracking Crime Rates**: This allowed them to see where offenses were highest, where watch patrols might need reinforcement, or whether new laws were effective.
- **Implications for Policing**: Though rudimentary, this was a step toward more evidence-based decision-making, moving away from ad hoc measures.

4.3. Professionalism among Officials

As Enlightenment values penetrated ruling circles, some states realized that incompetent or corrupt local enforcers undermined their authority. Hence, a movement toward:

- **Better Training**: Select police or judicial officers received rudimentary training in legal principles.
- **Specialized Roles**: Some cities created positions specifically dedicated to investigating crimes, though still not a modern detective force.
- **Uniforms and Identification**: In a few locales, watchmen or guard units wore distinctive clothing or badges, reinforcing the idea of an official, publicly accountable role.

5. Political Upheavals and Policing

5.1. The American Revolution (1775–1783)

Enlightenment ideas about rights, representation, and justified rebellion influenced the American colonies in their fight against British rule. While policing in the early United States would not fully formalize until the 19th century, the Revolution's rhetoric echoed Locke's notions of government by consent. After independence, American states adapted the old sheriff-constable system but combined it with republican ideals. This approach shaped early discourse on limiting the power of law enforcement while still maintaining public safety.

5.2. The French Revolution (1789–1799)

The French Revolution had a profound impact on policing concepts:

- **Destruction of Royal Institutions**: Revolutionaries abolished many old offices and tried to create a national guard or citizen militia reflecting popular sovereignty.
- **Declaration of the Rights of Man and of the Citizen**: This document enshrined principles of freedom, equality, and due process, challenging arbitrary policing.
- **New Police Bodies**: Revolutionaries established elected local officials to supervise safety, though revolutionary turmoil eventually led to the Committee of Public Safety, which ironically used draconian measures to root out "enemies of the revolution."

Although the revolution took policing in complex and sometimes contradictory directions, it represented a significant break from absolute monarchy's top-down control, injecting Enlightenment ideals directly into governance.

6. Enlightened Despots and Partial Reforms

6.1. Catherine the Great of Russia

Catherine corresponded with Voltaire and Diderot, earning a reputation as an "enlightened despot." She promoted legal codification and sought to reduce judicial abuses. Yet her reforms were limited by practical concerns: retaining nobility support, controlling vast territories, and stifling peasant revolts. Policing thus remained a patchwork of local gentry's authority, Cossack patrols, and an evolving bureaucracy in urban centers like St. Petersburg. Her efforts reflected the tension between progressive ideals and autocratic reality.

6.2. Joseph II of Austria

Joseph II attempted sweeping reforms across the Habsburg domains. He abolished serfdom (in principle), introduced religious toleration, and rationalized administrative structures. Policing under Joseph II aimed for more systematic oversight, with officials expected to follow uniform procedures. Nonetheless, local traditions and resistance from powerful interests curbed his reach, and many reforms were rolled back after his death.

6.3. Frederick the Great of Prussia

Frederick the Great championed a form of "enlightened absolutism," maintaining strict control while espousing some Enlightenment ideas. He was known to personally review judicial cases and insisted on certain humane standards, banning torture in most instances. Prussia's bureaucracy under Frederick became increasingly efficient, and policing benefitted from clearer lines of authority. However, underlying the enlightened veneer was a military-focused regime that suppressed deep democratic impulses.

7. Censorship, Freedom of the Press, and Policing

7.1. Controlling the Printed Word

While Enlightenment thinkers called for freedom of expression, most 18th-century governments maintained censorship laws. Police agencies or officials could seize seditious literature, arrest authors or printers, and shut down newspapers. Despite this, an underground culture of pamphlets and clandestine books flourished, eroding the monopoly of official state narratives.

7.2. Coffeehouses and Salons

Urban centers saw the rise of **coffeehouses** and **salons**—spaces where citizens and intellectuals debated politics, philosophy, and current events. These gatherings sometimes attracted police attention, especially if conversation turned critical of the monarch or the church. Spies or informers might frequent these venues, reporting subversive talk. Yet the proliferation of such public forums showed that Enlightenment ideas were becoming harder to contain.

7.3. Shifting Attitudes on Dissent

A slow shift occurred in how dissent was policed. Instead of brute force alone, monarchs and officials recognized the need to manage public opinion. They might release or reduce punishments for certain critics, hoping to appear magnanimous, or engage in propaganda to counter dangerous ideas. This more nuanced approach suggested an evolving concept of state power—one that recognized popular sentiment, at least to some degree.

8. International Exchange of Ideas

8.1. Grand Tours and Diplomatic Visits

Wealthy Europeans undertook "Grand Tours," traveling across the continent to broaden their education. Princes, ministers, and scholars visited courts and observed different policing systems firsthand. These travels fostered an exchange of Enlightenment ideas, including debates about the role of law enforcement in society.

8.2. Translations and Intellectual Networks

Works by Beccaria, Montesquieu, and Voltaire circulated widely. Translations reached Russia, the Americas, and beyond. Intellectual clubs, Masonic lodges, and academies discussed reforms to criminal law and policing. Though immediate change was rare, these dialogues eroded the old assumption that the king's word was law, offering new visions of structured, rational governance.

9. Limitations and Contradictions of Enlightenment Policing

9.1. Persistence of Inequality

Enlightenment reforms primarily served the interests of middle-class and noble elites. Peasants and laborers often remained subject to local lords or faced harsh city ordinances. Racial and colonial injustices continued; for instance, Enlightenment ideals rarely extended to enslaved peoples in the colonies, where policing remained brutal and coercive (as discussed in Chapter 8).

9.2. Partial Implementations

Many "enlightened" rulers cherry-picked reforms. They might abolish torture but keep widespread censorship, or champion religious tolerance while suppressing political dissent. Genuine accountability for police actions was minimal, as independent courts or legislatures capable of challenging royal decisions were rare.

9.3. Setbacks and Backlashes

Some reforms triggered backlash from conservative forces (the church, old nobility) or from local populations who preferred familiar customs. The Enlightenment's push for rational policing often clashed with deeply ingrained traditions of communal justice, patron-client relationships, and deference to local elites.

Chapter 11

Napoleonic Influence and the Spread of Police Institutions

In the preceding chapters, we explored how Enlightenment ideas began reshaping views on justice, punishment, and policing. We also noted how revolutionary upheavals—especially in France—sparked debates about the role of law enforcement in a changing society. Now, we turn our attention to **Napoleon Bonaparte** (1769–1821) and the significant influence his regime had on policing structures across Europe and beyond.

Napoleon's rise to power brought a mix of military discipline, administrative efficiency, and a personal ambition to control vast territories. Under the Consulate (1799–1804) and then the Empire (1804–1814), France saw the development and export of new legal and bureaucratic systems. The famous **Napoleonic Code** (Code Civil) codified civil law, setting a model for many other nations. Alongside this legal unification, Napoleon's government bolstered the tools of **internal security**—secret police, centralized administrations, and local officials loyal to the regime.

In this chapter, we will examine:

1. How Napoleon's government reorganized police institutions in France, building on revolutionary changes but also reintroducing strong central control.
2. The formation of the **Prefecture of Police** in Paris and the role of the Ministry of General Police.
3. Napoleon's use of a **secret police network** and censorship to monitor opponents and enforce loyalty.
4. How the Napoleonic Wars spread French administrative ideas—especially policing methods—across much of Europe.
5. Reactions by other states—both collaborators and resisters—to Napoleonic policing, and how these influenced later reforms.
6. The long-term legacy of Napoleon's administrative model, which continued to shape European policing long after his defeat.

By exploring these developments, we see that Napoleon's era was critical in shifting law enforcement toward a more **state-organized, bureaucratic** form, combining Enlightenment rationality with autocratic impulses. This tension—between centralized authority and ideals of civil rights—remained at the heart of European policing debates throughout the 19th century.

1. France after the Revolution: Setting the Stage

1.1. Revolutionary Police Experiments

The French Revolution (1789-1799) dismantled many of the **Ancien Régime** institutions, including the old royal police structure in Paris. Revolutionary leaders created new bodies—municipal police forces, committees of public safety, national guard units, and local citizen patrols—trying to ensure that the people, rather than a king, were in charge of security.

However, these structures often clashed or overlapped. During the most radical phase (the Terror, 1793-1794), policing became a tool of the Committee of Public Safety, which used draconian methods to hunt for "enemies of the revolution." After the fall of Robespierre, France saw a more moderate Directory government (1795-1799), but policing remained fragmented. Different factions, royalist conspirators, and external threats all competed for influence, making it difficult for the Directory to maintain control.

1.2. Napoleon's Rise to Power

Amidst this unstable political environment, **Napoleon Bonaparte**—a successful military general—staged the coup of 18 Brumaire (1799) and established the

Consulate, soon naming himself First Consul. He skillfully used his popularity with the army, along with public fatigue from years of turmoil, to gain near-dictatorial powers. Recognizing that his regime depended on securing public order, Napoleon began reorganizing France's administrative and policing apparatus to ensure loyalty and efficiency.

2. Centralizing the Police: The Ministry of General Police

2.1. Creation and Purpose

Under the Consulate, Napoleon formalized the **Ministry of General Police** (Ministère de la Police générale). Although roots of this office date back to Revolutionary policing attempts, Napoleon gave it broader powers and a clearer hierarchy:

- **Oversight of Local Forces**: The ministry coordinated the activities of local police in towns and cities across France.
- **Espionage and Counter-Subversion**: A key function was monitoring political dissidents, émigrés, and potential royalist or Jacobin conspiracies.
- **Surveillance of Public Opinion**: The ministry gathered information on what newspapers wrote, what people said in cafes, and how citizens responded to government policies.

2.2. Key Figures: Fouché and Savary

Two figures played central roles in shaping Napoleonic policing:

1. **Joseph Fouché** (Minister of Police from 1799 to 1810, with some interruptions): Originally a radical Jacobin, Fouché proved adept at manipulating political currents. Under Napoleon, he built a vast network of spies and informants. He excelled at balancing the emperor's demand for control with the need to maintain at least a veneer of public tolerance.
2. **Anne Jean Marie René Savary** (Duc de Rovigo), who replaced Fouché in 1810: A loyal Napoleonic officer, he emphasized discipline and direct subordination to Napoleon. Under Savary, policing became even more militarized, focusing on preventing any form of dissent.

Fouché and Savary demonstrated how personal loyalty and a willingness to implement strict surveillance were key to running the Ministry of General Police. Their approach combined cunning diplomacy with firm control, ensuring Napoleon had advance notice of opposition and could swiftly suppress threats.

2.3. Tools and Methods

To achieve these goals, the ministry used:

- **Informants and Agents**: Thousands of paid informants, from tavern keepers to petty criminals, reported on suspicious behavior.
- **Interception of Mail**: Police agents routinely opened letters to track conspiracies or gauge public sentiment.
- **Press Censorship**: Newspapers needed licenses to operate, and critical journalists faced harassment or closure.
- **Travel Controls**: Passports or official papers were sometimes required for internal movement, particularly for those suspected of anti-government activities.

While these measures solidified Napoleon's rule, they also disturbed many who remembered the Revolution's call for liberty. Yet, with ongoing war and fear of internal chaos, many French citizens accepted heightened surveillance as a trade-off for stability.

3. The Prefecture of Police in Paris

3.1. Historical Background

Paris had long been a center for policing innovation under the Ancien Régime. The **Lieutenant Général de Police** office, established in the 17th century, had made Paris's police one of the most famous in Europe. But the Revolution initially swept away this old royal structure.

3.2. Founding the Prefecture (1800)

In March 1800, Napoleon and his government established the **Prefecture of Police** in Paris. This new office replaced the chaotic Revolutionary organizations with a single authority overseeing:

- **Urban Order**: Maintaining public safety, firefighting, traffic regulation, and cleanliness in the sprawling capital.
- **Crime Prevention and Investigation**: Gathering intelligence on criminals, organizing patrols, and cooperating with the Ministry of General Police on serious cases.
- **Regulatory Functions**: Overseeing markets, businesses, and guilds, ensuring they complied with regulations that promoted public order and state interests.

3.3. The Prefect's Role

The **Prefect of Police** was appointed by the government, typically someone with proven loyalty. This official had sweeping powers, controlling a sizable force of inspectors, constables, and administrative staff. The prefect also worked closely with the Ministry of General Police, passing on intelligence and receiving directives to clamp down on potential unrest.

Under Napoleon, the Paris police became a model for centralized urban law enforcement—disciplined, hierarchical, and strongly tied to the executive branch. This concept of a **city-based police** under direct government authority influenced future reforms in France and abroad, showcasing how a capital's police could be used to demonstrate the regime's strength and efficiency.

4. Military Influence on Policing

4.1. Soldiers as Police

Napoleon's background as a military commander colored his approach to policing. He believed in hierarchy, discipline, and swift action. Throughout France, army officers or ex-officers often held positions in police administration. In smaller towns, **gendarmerie** units acted as both local police and internal security forces. The gendarmes were uniformed and structured along military lines, reporting to the central government.

4.2. Gendarmerie and Rural Control

Initially formed during the French Revolution to replace the royal Maréchaussée, the **gendarmerie** was further reorganized under Napoleon. Each department (the French term for regional districts) had its gendarmerie brigade, responsible for:

- **Patrolling Roads**: Ensuring safe travel and preventing highway robberies.
- **Suppressing Smuggling and Banditry**: Seizing contraband, especially as the Continental System (Napoleon's blockade against Britain) demanded tight border controls.
- **Supporting Local Officials**: Helping prefects and sub-prefects keep order.
- **Tracking Deserters**: Since France was almost perpetually at war, capturing deserting soldiers was critical.

The gendarmerie's mix of military rigor and police duty became a blueprint for rural policing in several later European states. Their presence in the countryside reinforced the sense that Napoleon's administration reached even the most remote villages.

5. Export of Napoleonic Models Across Europe

5.1. The Grand Empire

At the height of Napoleon's power, France dominated or directly controlled large swaths of Europe—Italy, the Low Countries, parts of Germany, the Grand Duchy of Warsaw, and more. In these satellite states or allied kingdoms, Napoleon's administrators introduced French-style legal and policing frameworks:

1. **Napoleonic Code**: Civil law that replaced feudal or patchwork local laws, emphasizing clarity and the equality of citizens before the law (though often with exceptions for the Emperor's needs).
2. **Centralized Administration**: Departments or provinces run by prefects or governors loyal to Napoleon.
3. **Gendarmerie or Similar Forces**: Sometimes new paramilitary police units, often staffed by local recruits but commanded by French officers.

5.2. Collaboration vs. Resistance

Local elites in conquered or allied territories reacted differently:

- **Collaboration**: Some reform-minded figures welcomed the Napoleonic system, believing it more rational and efficient than their previous feudal

structures. They might staff the police forces and prefectures with local supporters of Napoleon, hoping to modernize governance.
- **Resistance**: Traditional aristocracies, clergy, or nationalist groups often hated French domination. They saw the new police as an occupying force. Secret societies or guerrilla bands formed to harass these authorities. Police in these areas had to deal with sabotage, espionage, and popular uprisings—mirroring the challenges faced by France's own Ministry of General Police.

5.3. Long-Term Influence

Though Napoleon's empire eventually collapsed, many states retained elements of French administrative style. The standardization of law, the notion of a **prefect**, and the use of state-run police forces endured, shaping reforms in post-Napoleonic Europe. Even after the Congress of Vienna (1814–1815) restored older monarchies, the seed of central bureaucracy and codified legal structures had been planted.

6. The Secret Police and Surveillance Abroad

6.1. Napoleon's European Spy Network

Beyond France's borders, Napoleon relied on spies to gather intelligence on allied rulers, local populations, and enemy nations. Agents disguised themselves as merchants or travelers. They reported on local politics and sentiments, providing the emperor with vital information to preempt rebellions or plan military strategies. This emphasis on intelligence gathering underscored how policing and espionage had merged in Napoleonic governance.

6.2. Impact on Other Powers

Rival states recognized the effectiveness of Napoleon's intelligence efforts. Britain, Austria, Prussia, and Russia all sought to enhance their own spy services, though each had different approaches. Some introduced or strengthened their own political police units, worried about pro-Napoleonic sympathies among their populations. This arms race in covert policing set a precedent for the 19th century, where governments increasingly saw espionage as a standard tool of statecraft.

7. Censorship and Propaganda

7.1. Tight Control Over Information

Napoleon famously said that four hostile newspapers were more dangerous than a thousand bayonets. He thus kept a firm grip on the press. In France:

- **Newspapers**: The number of permitted newspapers shrank drastically. Those that remained were censored to promote Napoleon's achievements and stifle dissent.
- **Books and Pamphlets**: Publishers had to obtain licenses. Unapproved works risked confiscation or their authors faced arrests.
- **Propaganda Machine**: Official bulletins and state-sponsored newspapers glorified Napoleon's victories, shaping public opinion to see him as a heroic figure of order and stability.

7.2. Extending Censorship to Annexed Territories

French-controlled regions experienced similar censorship regimes. Local papers were pressured to praise Napoleon's administration, or at least refrain from criticizing it. Secret printing presses, smuggled pamphlets, and word-of-mouth networks emerged among resistance groups. This interplay between strict policing and covert resistance foreshadowed later 19th-century battles over free expression and the role of the state in regulating speech.

8. Challenges and Setbacks in Policing the Empire

8.1. Overextension and Local Revolts

Napoleon's campaigns stretched from Spain to Russia. Policing such a vast empire proved daunting:

- **Peninsular War in Spain (1808–1814)**: Guerrilla warfare and anti-French sentiment forced the French army and local police authorities into brutal reprisals. Instead of stable control, the region descended into continuous conflict.
- **Difficult Terrains**: In mountainous or rural areas of central Europe, local partisans frequently harassed garrisons, complicating the job of Napoleonic police and gendarmerie.

- **Resource Strain**: As wars dragged on, France struggled to maintain well-funded and loyal police forces everywhere. Desertion, corruption, and heavy casualties took a toll.

8.2. Internal Opposition in France

Even within France, dissatisfaction grew over conscription demands, heavy taxation, and restrictions on civil liberties. Though Napoleon's police attempted to quell unrest, it could not entirely hide the empire's mounting problems. As military defeats piled up (most notably the disastrous Russian campaign of 1812), the aura of invincibility around Napoleon faded, emboldening critics.

The End of the Empire and Aftermath

9.1. The Bourbon Restoration

After Napoleon's initial abdication in 1814, the **Bourbons** returned to the French throne. Louis XVIII kept some of the Napoleonic police frameworks, recognizing their administrative value. However, the political climate changed—royalists wanted to purge Napoleonic loyalists from influential positions, while some liberals sought greater freedoms. Policing thus entered a transitional period, juggling old Napoleonic methods with new political demands.

9.2. The Hundred Days and Final Defeat

Napoleon's brief return to power in 1815 (the Hundred Days) saw him attempt to rally French support one last time. He restored some of his earlier police apparatus but faced widespread European opposition. After defeat at Waterloo, Napoleon was exiled for good. Many of his top police officials were dismissed or went into hiding, fearing royal retribution.

9.3. Congress of Vienna and the Concert of Europe

The **Congress of Vienna** reorganized the continent, aiming for a balance of power to prevent another Napoleonic-style conquest. In policing terms, many states recognized the utility of strong central administrations. Some retained gendarmerie-like forces, while others reestablished older structures with minor modifications. The push for liberal constitutions and civil liberties grew slowly, clashing with conservative monarchies that used Napoleonic-style policing for their own ends.

10. The Long-Term Legacy of Napoleonic Policing

10.1. Administrative Centralization

Napoleon's rule demonstrated how a well-structured bureaucracy, combined with loyal policing, could unify a large state. The notion of a **central ministry** overseeing police forces at the national level influenced later European governments. Even states that despised Napoleon recognized the administrative efficiency of a single command hierarchy rather than fragmented feudal or local systems.

10.2. Codified Laws and a Professionalized Force

The **Napoleonic Code** spread the concept that laws should be clear, accessible, and relatively uniform. This idea complemented the professionalization of policing: well-defined laws needed equally clear policing procedures. While corruption persisted, the principle of having trained officers, official ranks, and standard practices gained acceptance across many countries in the 19th century.

10.3. Balancing Security with Liberties

Napoleonic policing was undoubtedly authoritarian. Yet it clashed with the ideals of the Revolution and Enlightenment, which advocated civil rights and due process. This conflict became a cornerstone of later debates: how could governments maintain order without trampling on individual freedoms? For many 19th-century thinkers and reformers, Napoleon's methods served as both a model of efficiency and a warning of potential tyranny.

10.4. Influence on Future Policing Models

The next decades would see major changes in policing—especially in Britain, where Robert Peel's efforts would create a new kind of municipal force in 1829 (the Metropolitan Police). Even so, Napoleonic-era ideas about a uniformed, state-directed police influenced many continental countries as they developed their own forces. Some borrowed heavily from the gendarmerie system for rural areas, and from the prefecture model for cities.

Chapter 12

Policing in the Early 19th Century

In Chapter 11, we discussed Napoleon's centralization of policing and how his methods influenced many European states. By the early 19th century (roughly the period from 1815 to the 1840s), Europe was undergoing significant transformations. The **Congress of Vienna** (1814–1815) attempted to stabilize the continent by restoring monarchies and creating a "Concert of Europe" to prevent large-scale wars. Meanwhile, **industrialization** began reshaping society in Britain, parts of Germany, and beyond, increasing urban populations and creating new social challenges.

Amid these changes, governments recognized the need for more systematic and professional policing. The older models—feudal watch systems, rural militias, or purely military garrisons—were proving inadequate in the face of **rising crime**, **public unrest**, and the complexities of growing cities. Napoleon's example, combined with Enlightenment ideas and new political pressures, led to experiments in policing that laid the groundwork for what we might call "modern" law enforcement—although true modern policing would emerge in the mid-19th century and beyond.

In this chapter, we will explore:

1. Post-Napoleonic Europe's political environment and its impact on law enforcement.
2. The continued use of secret police and censorship by conservative regimes, aiming to thwart liberal or nationalist uprisings.
3. Britain's unique path to early policing reforms, culminating in Sir Robert Peel's creation of the **Metropolitan Police** in 1829.
4. Parallel developments in continental Europe—Austria, Prussia, and smaller states—where rulers balanced Napoleonic influences with local traditions.
5. The role of industrialization and urban migration in shaping public safety concerns, leading to new policing methods.
6. Tensions between those demanding civil liberties and the states seeking order, setting the stage for future reforms.

By the end of this chapter, we will see that early 19th-century policing was a **transition period**, bridging the post-revolutionary autocratic measures of

Napoleon with emerging liberal demands for accountable, professional law enforcement.

1. The Post-Napoleonic Political Climate

1.1. The Congress of Vienna and the Restoration

After Napoleon's final defeat at Waterloo (1815), European powers met at the **Congress of Vienna** to restore the pre-revolutionary order. Kings and princes returned to their thrones, determined to prevent another revolutionary wave. However, the transformations of the previous decades could not simply be undone:

- **Administrative Structures**: Many states retained the centralized bureaucracy introduced under French domination.
- **Legal Codes**: Napoleonic or Enlightenment-influenced codes remained in effect, with modifications.
- **Policing Institutions**: Gendarmerie units, secret police, and censorial practices persisted, though often under different leadership.

1.2. The Holy Alliance and Conservative Policing

Tsar Alexander I of Russia, Emperor Francis I of Austria, and King Frederick William III of Prussia formed the **Holy Alliance**, pledging to uphold Christian and monarchical principles. Metternich, the Austrian foreign minister, became a leading figure in suppressing liberal or nationalist movements. This suppression often involved:

- **Secret Police Networks**: Gathering intelligence on student fraternities, liberal clubs, or any group advocating constitutionalism.
- **Censorship**: Restricting newspapers, books, and lectures that criticized the monarchy or promoted "dangerous" ideas.
- **Coordinated Actions**: States occasionally cooperated to crush revolts (like the Carbonari uprisings in Italy), using both armies and local police to arrest leaders and break up conspiracies.

These actions reflected a conservative mindset worried about another revolution. Policing methods thus skewed toward maintaining the status quo rather than embracing liberal reforms.

2. Rising Social Pressures: Urbanization and Crime

2.1. Industrialization and City Growth

While Britain led the Industrial Revolution, other parts of Europe also experienced gradual industrial expansion. Urban centers grew quickly, drawing rural migrants seeking factory work. This population boom triggered:

- **Overcrowded Housing**: Slums emerged, lacking sanitation and basic infrastructure.
- **Poor Working Conditions**: Long hours, low wages, and minimal safety measures contributed to social tension.
- **Visible Poverty**: Begging, petty theft, and homelessness became more common in dense city districts.

Traditional watchmen, typically few in number and amateur in training, struggled to cope with these challenges. Local merchants, property owners, and reform-minded citizens began calling for more **organized policing** to reduce crime and control vagrancy or riots.

2.2. The Perceived Crime Wave

Sensational stories of robberies, burglaries, and violent assaults circulated in newspapers, fueling public fear. Though historical crime data is patchy, the sense of a "crime wave" was widespread in early industrial cities:

- **Gangs and Pickpockets**: Crowded markets and narrow streets provided ideal conditions for pickpockets. Organized gangs might form in urban underworlds.
- **Riots and Protests**: Workers sometimes rioted against wage cuts or mechanization they believed would steal their jobs (e.g., the Luddite movement in Britain). Local militias or troops often suppressed these incidents violently.
- **Moral Panic**: Middle-class observers complained about "loose morals" in slum districts, believing better policing would instill discipline and deter vice.

This environment pushed policymakers to consider new policing frameworks that went beyond occasional military intervention or local watch patrols.

3. Britain's Path to Policing Reform

3.1. Early Attempts: The Thames River Police and Bow Street Runners

Before Sir Robert Peel's reforms, Britain had some notable policing experiments:

1. **Bow Street Runners** (founded mid-18th century by Henry Fielding): A small group of paid constables in London who investigated crimes and pursued offenders. They built a reputation for efficiency, but their limited numbers could not cover all of London.

2. **Thames River Police** (1798): Funded by merchants to reduce theft on the docks, this force demonstrated that a specialized, salaried, and uniformed police presence could significantly reduce crime.

3.2. Mounting Pressure for Change

By the 1820s, London's population exceeded one million. Street lighting, sewers, and public health measures lagged far behind. Crime concerns escalated:

- **Pickpocketing and Mugging**: Crowded slums and dimly lit alleys provided cover for criminals.
- **Public Drunkenness**: Gin drinking was rampant, adding to social disorder.
- **Ineffectiveness of the Night Watch**: Part-time watchmen, often poorly paid and unmotivated, were ill-equipped to handle rising crime.

Merchants and reformers feared London's situation would damage trade and undermine civic life. Meanwhile, some members of Parliament worried that centralizing police might threaten English traditions of local governance and personal liberties, reminiscent of the perceived French-style "police state."

3.3. Sir Robert Peel and the Metropolitan Police (1829)

Sir Robert Peel, serving as Home Secretary, introduced the **Metropolitan Police Act** in 1829. It created a full-time, professional police force for the Greater London area (excluding the City of London, which retained its own separate force). Key elements:

- **Uniformed Officers (Peelers or Bobbies)**: Easily identifiable uniforms (blue tailcoats and top hats) aimed to present a non-military appearance, reassuring the public that they were not soldiers.
- **Central Headquarters (Scotland Yard)**: Command structure with commissioners overseeing divisions, each responsible for specific city areas.
- **Peelian Principles**: Emphasized crime prevention through visible patrols rather than just responding after crimes occurred. Police legitimacy, Peel argued, depended on public approval and minimal use of force.

Though resistance existed—some saw it as a step toward tyranny—Londoners gradually accepted the new force. Crime rates in patrolled areas appeared to decline, and the concept of a neutral, professional police gained traction.

3.4. Spreading the "New Police" Model

Over the next decade, many British towns and cities adopted or adapted the Metropolitan model, passing local acts to form police boards or commissioners. By 1856 (beyond our current chapter's main range but worth noting briefly), Parliament made it mandatory for all counties to establish professional forces. Peel's initiative thus shaped policing not only in Britain but influenced forces in Canada, Australia, and other parts of the British Empire. Even continental nations watched Britain's experiment with interest, though they blended it with their own bureaucratic traditions.

4. Continental Europe: Between Napoleon and Liberal Revolutions

4.1. Austria and the Metternich System

As foreign minister and later chancellor, **Klemens von Metternich** (1773–1859) became synonymous with post-Napoleonic conservatism. He used policing to thwart liberalism and nationalism, especially in the German Confederation:

- **Carlsbad Decrees (1819)**: Issued after student demonstrations in Germany, these decrees censored the press and empowered universities to expel activists. Police tracked professors and students suspected of radical ideas.
- **Secret Police**: Operatives reported on political clubs, newspapers, and public gatherings. Potential revolutionaries were arrested or forced into exile.
- **Local Armies and Gendarmerie**: In the Habsburg lands, military units sometimes doubled as police, particularly in rural areas.

Though the Metternich System was effective in delaying revolutionary outbreaks, it could not eliminate the underlying social and political pressures that exploded across Europe in 1848.

4.2. Prussia and Other German States

Prussia, having absorbed Napoleonic lessons, maintained a disciplined bureaucracy and an extended **gendarmerie**:

- **Rural Patrols**: Gendarmes covered the countryside, often forming the backbone of local policing.
- **Urban Police**: Major cities like Berlin developed watch forces, but calls for modernization grew as industrialization advanced in the Rhine provinces.
- **Political Surveillance**: Prussian authorities monitored nationalist student groups (the Burschenschaften). Officials worried these educated youth could spark unrest aiming for German unification.

Smaller German states varied in approach. Some embraced minor constitutional reforms but still relied on censorship and covert policing to curb dissent.

4.3. Italy's Patchwork

Italy remained fragmented under Austrian influence, the Papal States, the Kingdom of Sardinia-Piedmont, the Bourbon monarchy in Naples, and various duchies. Each region had different policing traditions:

- **Papal States**: The papal government maintained a mix of Swiss Guards, local militias, and a secret police apparatus to stamp out liberal or anti-clerical agitation.
- **Northern Italy**: Austrian officials and local elites clashed with carbonari secret societies calling for independence. Police infiltration of these groups was widespread, leading to arrests and exiles.
- **Kingdom of Sardinia-Piedmont**: This region started modest administrative reforms, including police reorganization, hoping to strengthen the monarchy's grip while placating moderate reformers.

Lack of uniformity across the peninsula mirrored the broader fragmentation of Italy. However, a shared anti-Austrian sentiment and desire for modernization stirred nationalist movements that the local police struggled to contain.

5. Policing in an Age of Revolts (1820s–1840s)

5.1. Revolutions in the 1820s

In the early 1820s, a wave of uprisings occurred in Spain, Portugal, and parts of Italy, driven by demands for constitutional rule. While many were suppressed with help from the Holy Alliance, they highlighted:

- **Police Shortcomings**: The reliance on military intervention indicated local police forces often could not handle large-scale political revolts.

- **Growing Liberal Networks**: Secret societies or "underground" printing presses evaded censors. Police spent significant resources chasing conspirators, revealing how policing had become deeply tied to political control.

5.2. The July Revolution (1830) in France

The Bourbon restoration (1814–1830) ended when Charles X tried to curb press freedoms and dissolve Parliament. Parisians rebelled, toppling the regime in the **July Revolution** of 1830. This event:

- **Reshaped French Policing**: The new "July Monarchy" under Louis-Philippe maintained the Prefecture of Police but moderated some censorship.
- **Inspiration Abroad**: Revolutions flared in Belgium (leading to independence from the Netherlands) and uprisings in Italy and Poland. Local police, often outnumbered or unprepared, leaned again on army support to restore order.
- **Balancing Act**: Louis-Philippe's government tried to balance liberal reforms with a strong police apparatus, hoping to avoid radical upheaval.

5.3. The Road to 1848

Throughout the 1830s and 1840s, pressures mounted—economic downturns, bad harvests, and the spread of radical newspapers fueled discontent. Policing grew more complex:

- **Urban Worker Movements**: In industrial centers (like Lyon in France, or the coal regions of Prussia), laborers began organizing strikes or protests. Police infiltration of worker groups became common, but not always successful.
- **Middle-Class Demands**: A rising bourgeoisie demanded constitutional freedoms and expanded suffrage. They resented heavy-handed policing, especially censorship.
- **Nationalism**: Poles under Russian rule, Hungarians within the Habsburg empire, and Italians under foreign domination agitated for independence. Police monitored these nationalist cells, often labeling them subversives.

By the mid-1840s, many European police forces faced tasks far beyond routine law enforcement—suppressing potential revolts, navigating censorship demands, and dealing with a restless public shaped by industrial and ideological change.

6. Policing Innovations and Ideas

6.1. Professional Training

Inspired partly by Peel's success in London, some continental cities began offering limited **training programs** for recruits:

- **Use of Uniforms**: Uniformed patrols became more common, distinguishing professional police from amateur watchmen or military squads.
- **Record Keeping**: Officials tried to maintain registers of known criminals or political suspects, building on Napoleonic-era administrative practices.
- **Early Forensic Methods**: Although rudimentary, some police began collecting evidence from crime scenes, questioning witnesses systematically, and storing records for future reference.

6.2. Municipal vs. State Police

Debates arose over whether policing should be locally controlled (municipal police) or centrally directed by the state (as under Napoleon). Opinions split along political lines:

- **Liberals**: Often favored local or municipal oversight, believing it would reduce abuses of power and reflect community needs.
- **Conservatives**: Preferred a strong central authority, worried that local officials might show leniency to radicals or fail to protect the monarchy.
- **Compromises**: Some states used a hybrid approach, allowing local funding for police but requiring officers to follow guidelines set by a central ministry of the interior or police.

6.3. The Growth of Detective Units

Though formal detective bureaus (like the later Paris Sûreté) or specialized inquiry branches were still in their infancy, some big cities experimented with plainclothes officers. These early detectives primarily tracked serious criminals (burglars, counterfeiters) and political enemies. The tension between uniformed public patrols and secretive detective work symbolized broader policing dilemmas: transparency vs. undercover efficiency.

7. Policing Beyond Europe

7.1. North American Developments

In the United States and Canada, many transplanted the **sheriff-constable** system from England. Growing cities like New York and Toronto recognized the need for more structured forces. By the 1830s and 1840s, New York began experimenting with a day watch and a night watch, eventually merging them into a single police department (though the major reorganization happened in the mid-19th century).

7.2. Latin America

Newly independent states in Latin America (former Spanish colonies) often inherited Spanish-style policing—municipal guards, rural militias, and a legacy of strong central authority. Political instability, civil wars, and caudillo (strongman) rule meant that policing fluctuated between local vigilante justice and militarized crackdowns. Enlightenment ideals or Napoleonic models influenced some liberal reformers, but these efforts were hampered by ongoing internal strife.

7.3. Colonial Possessions

European powers continued to impose policing structures on their colonies. In British India, for instance, a rudimentary police system expanded under the East India Company to protect trade and quell local rebellions. Over time, aspects of Peel's methods filtered into colonial policing, though often with a top-down approach aimed at controlling indigenous populations rather than truly serving them.

8. The Tensions Between Control and Freedom

8.1. Civil Liberties Concerns

Early 19th-century liberals challenged repressive measures like censorship, arbitrary arrests, and the use of the military in policing. They argued for:

- **Habeas Corpus** or equivalent protections, ensuring individuals could not be detained without formal charges.
- **Judicial Oversight** of police actions.
- **Freedom of the Press** to hold authorities accountable.

8.2. Secret Police vs. Public Acceptance

Governments that heavily relied on covert surveillance often faced public backlash. Figures like Metternich became synonymous with reactionary oppression. Over time, moderate rulers realized that policing which seemed too secretive or brutal could provoke revolts. This tension nudged some states to adopt a more transparent, "public service" style of policing in urban areas, while still quietly maintaining spy networks for political threats.

8.3. Seeds of Reform

Though full liberalization was not immediate, the early 19th century laid groundwork for future reforms. Debates on balancing police power and individual rights—sparked by Enlightenment, fueled by the memory of Napoleonic authoritarianism, and shaped by social pressures—would intensify in the coming decades. By the 1840s, Europe stood on the brink of major upheavals that would test and transform these policing institutions yet again.

9. Approaching the Mid-19th Century: The Threshold of Change

9.1. Gathering Storms

Economic recession, failed harvests, and political dissatisfaction converged in the late 1840s. Cities grew larger, class tensions mounted, and liberal-nationalist ideologies spread quickly through clandestine publications. Police forces, whether local or centralized, found themselves monitoring radical clubs, labor organizations, and patriotic societies.

9.2. The 1848 Revolutions

Although the main wave of European revolutions in 1848–1849 slightly exceeds our chapter's time frame, the lead-up illustrates how police systems were already strained:

- **France**: Louis-Philippe's monarchy faced worker protests and republican plots. The Paris Police Prefecture, though fairly well organized, could not stem public frustration with corruption and inequality.
- **German States**: Metternich's apparatus in Austria, along with other German states, tried to crush liberal-national groups. Nonetheless, dissatisfaction with censorship and reactionary rule grew.
- **Italy**: Nationalists and constitutionalists conspired against Austrian dominance in Lombardy-Venetia and reactionary governments in the south.

The revolutions of 1848 would reveal how deeply intertwined policing and political power had become in Europe. Many police forces were unprepared for mass insurrections, prompting either partial concessions from rulers or brutal crackdowns—both shaping the next stage of police development.

Chapter 13

Policing in Non-European Regions (Africa, Asia, Middle East)

In the previous chapters, we focused heavily on Europe's experiences—ancient civilizations, medieval influences, Enlightenment ideas, Napoleonic reforms, and early 19th-century shifts. However, policing did not follow a single European path around the globe. Different regions—particularly in **Africa**, **Asia**, and the **Middle East**—had their own long-standing traditions, structures, and philosophies of law enforcement. Sometimes these systems evolved independently; other times, they interacted with or were reshaped by European colonial powers.

In this chapter, we will examine:

1. **African Policing Traditions** before and during early colonial encroachment, noting the interplay between indigenous methods and outside influence.
2. **The Ottoman Empire** and neighboring Middle Eastern lands, where policing combined religious authority, local governance, and, later, modernization efforts.
3. **Persia (Iran)** under the Qajar Dynasty and how it managed internal security in a context balancing tradition and outside pressures.
4. **China** during the late imperial era (Qing Dynasty), including its bureaucratic structures and challenges from foreign incursions.
5. **Japan** transitioning from feudal-era policing under the samurai class to early modernization in the mid- to late 19th century, influenced partly by Western examples.
6. Broader patterns of **trade route security**, religiously based policing functions, and the role of local power holders (tribal chiefs, religious leaders, or local strongmen) in maintaining order.

We will keep our focus on the era spanning from roughly the early modern period up through the late 19th century, occasionally touching on the early 20th century. By doing so, we can see how non-European societies balanced their inherited policing traditions with the increasing pressure of European influences, industrial transformations, and internal reform efforts.

1. African Policing Traditions and Early Colonial Impact

1.1. Precolonial Methods of Law Enforcement

Before significant European domination, Africa contained a vast array of governance structures: large empires (e.g., Mali, Songhai, Ethiopia), smaller kingdoms, city-states, and tribal societies. Their approaches to law enforcement varied:

- **Customary Law and Elders' Councils**: In many communities, respected elders or chiefs settled disputes, enforced communal norms, and punished crimes. Social sanctions like ostracism or fines in livestock were common.
- **Age-Grades and Warrior Societies**: Some cultures, such as the Maasai in East Africa, had "age-set" systems. Young warriors might patrol borders, guard livestock, and keep internal order as part of their coming-of-age responsibilities.
- **Religious or Spiritual Authority**: In certain kingdoms (e.g., the Yoruba states), priests or religious figures held influence in judicial matters, merging spiritual mandates with social regulations.

These structures aimed to preserve harmony in communities where kinship ties were strong, and loyalty to local leaders was a key social bond. While not "police" in the modern sense, these systems effectively maintained order according to local norms.

1.2. Islamic Influence in North and West Africa

From roughly the 7th century onward, Islam spread across North Africa and into parts of West Africa (the Sahel region). This brought **Sharia** principles and new roles akin to the Middle Eastern **muhtasib** (market inspector) or **qadi** (judge).

- **Market Supervision**: Religious officials ensured fair trade practices and proper conduct in public spaces.
- **Hisbah Systems**: Some Islamic societies established a form of "hisbah," referring to the moral and market oversight that combined religious duty with social enforcement.
- **Mixed Approaches**: Local sultans or emirs often blended Islamic law with preexisting customary traditions, creating a hybrid policing structure. For instance, the Sokoto Caliphate in what is now northern Nigeria had district and village officials who combined Sharia-based justice with local governance.

1.3. Early Colonial Contacts: Coastal Trading Posts

From the 15th century onward, Europeans built coastal trading forts—first the Portuguese, then the Dutch, British, French, and others. Initially, these enclaves did not deeply transform inland policing, but they established new dynamics:

- **Fort Security**: European powers stationed soldiers or guards mainly to protect trade (often in gold, ivory, and later enslaved people).
- **Influence on Local Rulers**: Some African coastal chiefs sought European arms or alliances, which changed local power balances. In some areas, local leaders might adopt more militarized methods to control raiding or protect trading routes.
- **Slave Raids and Policing**: The Atlantic slave trade triggered violent disruptions. Some African states grew more militarized to defend or expand raids on neighbors, drastically altering the role of local enforcers.

By the mid-19th century, as European powers intensified their "Scramble for Africa," deeper colonial policing structures emerged, though these expansions truly took shape at the end of the 19th century. Nevertheless, earlier African policing methods remained influential in many communities that resisted or adapted to European rule.

2. The Ottoman Empire and Neighboring Middle Eastern Lands

2.1. Classical Ottoman Policing

From the 14th to the 19th century, the **Ottoman Empire** governed vast territories across Southeast Europe, Anatolia, the Levant, and parts of North Africa. While the Ottoman system was complex, a few main features stand out:

- **Centralized Administration (Sublime Porte)**: The sultan's government issued imperial decrees, but local authorities, such as pashas or beys, managed day-to-day matters in provinces.
- **Janissaries**: Historically, this elite corps served not only as soldiers but also as internal enforcers in major cities like Istanbul. Over time, they became entangled in politics, sometimes acting as a powerful faction rather than a neutral police force.
- **Religious Courts (Sharia)**: Qadis (judges) oversaw legal disputes. Local watchmen or ward officials might bring offenders before qadis. Morality enforcement sometimes fell to religious authorities ensuring compliance with Islamic practices.

2.2. Tanzimat Reforms and Police Modernization

By the early 19th century, the Ottoman Empire faced internal decline and external pressure. Reformers launched the **Tanzimat** period (1839–1876), seeking to centralize and modernize governance:

- **New Police Forces**: Inspired partly by European models, the empire tried to create more professional urban police, distinct from the older Janissary-based system. After the Janissaries were disbanded in 1826, local gendarmerie units were introduced to handle both rural and urban order.
- **Administrative Councils**: Provincial governors gained clearer instructions on collecting taxes, enlisting police forces, and maintaining roads for better trade and security.

- **Legal Reforms**: Elements of European law were incorporated alongside Islamic law, including new penal codes that defined crimes and punishments more systematically.

Although many challenges persisted, these reforms laid a foundation for more structured policing in major Ottoman cities like Istanbul, Damascus, and Cairo (though Egypt gained semi-autonomous status under Muhammad Ali).

2.3. Policing in Other Middle Eastern Realms

Beyond the Ottoman sphere, smaller states and emirates—like those in the Arabian Peninsula—often relied on tribal-based enforcement. Local sheikhs or emirs used retinues of armed men to preserve security, sometimes guided by Islamic precepts. In Persia (Iran), Qajar rulers faced similar pressures to modernize policing, which we explore next.

3. Persia (Iran) under the Qajar Dynasty

3.1. Traditional Structures

Following the Safavid era, the **Qajar Dynasty** (established 1794) ruled Iran through local governors and tribal chieftains who owed allegiance to the shah. Law enforcement typically combined:

- **Tribal Militias**: In many regions, powerful tribes maintained internal order through customary codes, enforced by clan elders or chiefs.
- **Urban and Bazaar Regulation**: Cities like Tehran, Tabriz, and Isfahan had local officials (kelantar or darugheh) overseeing markets and public safety.
- **Religious Authority**: Shi'a clerics wielded influence on moral and legal matters, especially in family and religious disputes.

3.2. Encroaching Foreign Influence

Throughout the 19th century, Russia and Britain competed for influence in Persia, imposing treaties that limited Qajar sovereignty and introduced new economic dependencies. This foreign intrusion prompted some Persian reformers to call for modernizing administrative and policing systems to strengthen national unity.

3.3. Early Modernization Efforts

In the late 19th century, rulers like Naser al-Din Shah attempted partial reforms:

- **Centralized Gendarmerie**: The government tried to form a more systematic gendarmerie to secure trade routes and quell tribal rebellions.
- **European Advisers**: Some shahs invited European military and administrative experts to train Persian forces, though budget constraints and internal politics slowed progress.
- **Inconsistent Implementation**: Tribal leaders often resisted losing autonomy, while city dwellers feared heavier taxation or outside interference. Consequently, policing improvements remained patchy.

Despite these hurdles, by the early 20th century, Persia had laid the groundwork for a nascent central police apparatus, blending local tradition, clerical authority, and partial Western-style structures.

4. Late Imperial China: The Qing Dynasty

4.1. Traditional Bureaucratic Control

For centuries, China's imperial system—especially under the Ming and Qing dynasties—relied on a vast bureaucracy of scholar-officials (selected via the imperial exam system). Policing was one aspect of governance handled through:

- **Local Magistrates (Yamen)**: Each county had a magistrate responsible for civil administration, tax collection, and judicial proceedings. He employed constables (bǔkuài) and runners (yamen staff) to enforce orders, gather evidence, and arrest suspects.
- **Clan and Village Elders**: Beyond official channels, many disputes were settled informally by family heads or village elders, reducing the magistrate's workload.
- **Baojia System**: A centuries-old system grouping households into collectives for mutual surveillance and security. If one member committed a crime, the entire group could be held responsible for reporting or preventing it.

4.2. Challenges in the 19th Century

By the 19th century, the Qing Dynasty faced multiple crises:

- **Population Growth**: Rapid demographic expansion strained local resources.
- **Corruption**: Some magistrates and constables demanded bribes, fueling public resentment.
- **Foreign Pressure**: The Opium Wars (mid-19th century), unequal treaties, and growing foreign concessions in treaty ports undermined Qing authority.

Secret societies like the Triads or the White Lotus movement flourished in neglected regions, filling a vacuum of enforcement or offering alternative "protection" systems. The Qing government tried to modernize certain aspects of policing, but internal rebellions (e.g., Taiping Rebellion) and external invasions consumed much of its focus.

4.3. Early Self-Strengthening

From the 1860s onward, the **Self-Strengthening Movement** sought to adopt selective Western technology and military organization. While large-scale police reform lagged behind, some coastal cities (e.g., Shanghai) established joint Sino-foreign municipal police in the international concessions. These forces used Western equipment, uniforms, and methods—though they primarily protected foreign commercial interests.

In other major Qing cities, small steps included better training for yamen runners, modest pay increases to reduce corruption, and attempts to standardize criminal procedures. Such changes set precedents for more thorough reforms in the early 20th century (beyond our scope). Still, the tension between local autonomy, traditional bureaucracy, and modernizing impulses defined Qing policing challenges through the dynasty's final decades.

5. Japan's Transition from Feudal to Modern Policing

5.1. Tokugawa Shogunate and Samurai Control

From the early 17th to mid-19th century, Japan was governed by the **Tokugawa Shogunate**. The daimyo (feudal lords) controlled domains (han), and the samurai class enforced local order:

- **Samurai as Enforcers**: Samurai were the military aristocracy. In peacetime, many served as administrators or local "police" within their domain.
- **Machibugyō (Town Magistrates)**: In cities like Edo (Tokyo), Osaka, and Kyoto, appointed town magistrates had judicial and policing functions, aided by subordinates such as yoriki (samurai officers) and dōshin (foot police).
- **Emphasis on Hierarchy**: Samurai authority over commoners was absolute; punishments could be swift, especially if a commoner disrespected a samurai. Meanwhile, clan or guild-based self-regulation handled lesser disputes.

5.2. The Meiji Restoration (1868) and Modernizing Forces

In 1853, Commodore Perry's arrival ended Japan's self-imposed isolation, revealing the Shogunate's military and technological disadvantage. Internal turmoil led to the **Meiji Restoration** (1868), which toppled the Tokugawa regime and returned nominal power to the emperor. Rapid modernization efforts followed:

- **Centralized Governance**: The Meiji government dismantled feudal domains and established prefectures with governors appointed by Tokyo.

- **Police Bureau Creation**: Heavily influenced by French and later German models, the new leadership established a centralized police bureau. Samurai traditions were partially repurposed, turning some former warriors into police officers.
- **Gendarmerie System**: Like many continental influences, Japan introduced a gendarmerie-style force, especially to quell rural uprisings. By the late 19th century, the Japanese police had uniforms, ranks, and Western-style training.
- **Moral Regulation**: Reflecting Confucian and nationalistic ideals, the Meiji police enforced not only crime laws but also "civic morality," controlling public behavior and punishing those who disrupted the new social order.

5.3. Balancing Old and New

While the government strove to create a modern state apparatus, deep cultural norms persisted. Police had to respect local authority structures (village headmen, temple networks) yet enforce new edicts from Tokyo. Over time, Japan formed one of the most centralized and efficient police systems in Asia, paralleling some aspects of European states but rooted in the country's feudal heritage.

6. Broader Patterns: Trade Routes, Religious Authority, and Local Power

6.1. Securing Trade Routes

Across Africa, Asia, and the Middle East, controlling trade routes was a key policing function:

- **Caravanserais and Patrols**: Camel caravans crossing the Sahara or Silk Road corridors needed security against bandits. Governments or local warlords posted watchmen or patrols at strategic points (oases, mountain passes).
- **Port Cities**: Major ports along the Indian Ocean (e.g., Zanzibar, Muscat, Calicut) and East Asian maritime routes (Canton/Guangzhou, Nagasaki) enforced trade rules via harbor masters and guards to regulate incoming vessels and travelers.
- **European Colonies**: As European presence grew, naval patrols and custom officials were placed in coastal regions. This arrangement

sometimes merged local policing traditions with external legal frameworks, often skewed in favor of foreign merchants.

6.2. Religious and Ethical Underpinnings

Whether under Islamic, Confucian, Hindu, or other traditions, moral and spiritual guidelines often informed policing:

- **Mosque-Based Enforcement**: In some Muslim regions, the Friday mosque served as a hub for moral policing, with imams, muftis, or qadis guiding local watchers.
- **Hindu Kingdoms**: Temple complexes could sponsor guards to protect pilgrims and holy sites, as seen in parts of South Asia.
- **Confucian Values**: In China, Confucian ideals stressed communal harmony and respect for hierarchy. This shaped policing to focus on mediation, preventing disruptions to social order.

6.3. Local Strongmen and Tribal Chiefs

Even with formal state structures, local chiefs or strongmen often remained powerful:

- **Client-Patron Systems**: Villagers or town residents pledged loyalty to a chief, who, in turn, offered protection and conflict resolution.
- **Quasi-Private Enforcers**: Armed retinues might collect taxes, guard roads, or enforce the chief's justice, sometimes clashing with official police or imperial troops.
- **Resistance to Centralization**: Attempts by emerging states (Ottoman reforms, Meiji Restoration, or Qajar centralization) to curb local power triggered revolts or negotiated compromises, reflecting a tug-of-war between state consolidation and local autonomy.

7. The Late 19th Century: Rising European Influence and Internal Reforms

7.1. Intensified Colonial Expansion in Africa

By the late 19th century, European powers seized large swaths of Africa. Policing under colonial rule often meant:

- **Paramilitary Forces**: Colonial administrations formed "native police" units led by European officers, using them to suppress resistance and collect taxes.
- **Mixed Jurisdictions**: Africans frequently faced separate legal systems—one for Europeans (applying European laws) and another for "natives" (some version of customary law, though often heavily regulated).
- **Co-Optation of Traditional Leaders**: The British, for instance, employed "indirect rule," using existing chiefs for daily policing tasks but ensuring ultimate control rested with colonial officials.

While major conquests occurred in the late 1800s, the foundations were laid earlier, as we have seen in coastal enclaves and initial treaties.

7.2. Middle East Reforms under European Pressure

The Ottoman Empire, Egypt (under the Khedives), and Persia faced mounting foreign debts and interventions:

- **Dual Financial Control**: European creditors influenced local governments, pushing for stable policing to secure trade and investments.
- **Railway and Telegraph Infrastructure**: Policing extended along new rail lines, ensuring safe transport of goods. Gendarmes or specialized railway police emerged in some regions.
- **Socio-Political Unrest**: Nationalist movements—like the Young Ottomans, Egyptian nationalists, and various Persian constitutionalists—criticized the use of police to stifle dissent. This tension grew as modern communications spread protest ideas more rapidly.

7.3. Asia's Accelerated Change

In East Asia, the late 19th century brought:

- **China's Self-Strengthening and Sino-Foreign Forces**: Treaty ports ran municipal police combining Chinese recruits and foreign officers, fueling controversies over extraterritorial rights. Rural policing lagged behind, leaving large swaths of the countryside under local strongmen or bandits.
- **Japan's Meiji Consolidation**: After quelling samurai rebellions (like the Satsuma Rebellion, 1877), the Meiji state strengthened police authority to enforce new Western-style laws and quell labor unrest.

- **Expansion of Western Influence**: Missions, trade outposts, and foreign advisors continued to shape legal and policing reforms in regions like Siam (Thailand) or Korea, though these states negotiated partial modernization to maintain sovereignty.

8. Interplay with European Models and Indigenous Adaptations

8.1. Hybrid Systems

Many non-European rulers selectively adopted European policing methods—uniformed patrols, rank hierarchies, even detective branches—while preserving cultural norms:

- **Legal Duality**: Some areas introduced Western criminal codes for trade or foreign relations, but kept religious or customary courts for personal matters (marriage, inheritance).
- **Western Advisors, Local Context**: Advisors from France, Britain, or other powers might train a new city police force, but local constraints (budget, tribal conflicts, religious law) limited how fully these models were implemented.

8.2. Resistance and Rebellion

Everywhere, policing faced pushback if it was seen as a tool of foreign encroachment or an oppressive central government:

- **Peasant Revolts**: Excessive taxation or forced labor systems policed by newly formed gendarmeries often led to uprisings.
- **Urban Intellectuals**: Western-educated elites in places like Cairo, Istanbul, and Shanghai criticized heavy-handed censorship, arrests of dissenters, and an overall lack of civil rights.
- **Secret Societies**: In China, the Triads and anti-foreign groups like the Boxers (late 19th century) resisted modernization. In the Middle East, clandestine nationalist groups grew, clashing with official police or gendarmerie.

9. The Early 20th Century Horizon

By the turn of the 20th century, many African, Middle Eastern, and Asian regions had policing systems in flux. Old structures persisted in rural settings, with chiefs or clan elders dispensing local justice. Meanwhile, major cities—like Cairo, Istanbul, Tehran, Tokyo, and Shanghai—developed modern-style forces, influenced by Western ideas. Tensions between these dual or multiple layers of law enforcement often reflected deeper societal struggles over identity, governance, and independence.

Though comprehensive modernization of policing in these regions would often come well into the 20th century and beyond, the late 19th-century seeds were already planted. Patterns of centralized police, paramilitary gendarmerie, religious oversight, or local chief-based enforcement each responded to unique cultural contexts, shaped by the interplay of tradition and outside power.

Chapter 14

Early Policing in the United States

In the previous chapter, we examined policing across diverse non-European regions—Africa, Asia, and the Middle East—highlighting a blend of ancient customs, religious institutions, and selective modernization. Now, we turn to the **United States**, a nation whose earliest colonies sprang from British roots but soon developed distinct patterns of governance and law enforcement.

From the 17th century onward, the territories that became the United States experienced **frontier expansion, slavery, urbanization**, and deep political changes. These forces shaped American policing in ways that both resembled English systems (e.g., sheriffs, constables) and diverged into unique forms like **slave patrols**. By the early 19th century, as cities like New York, Boston, and Philadelphia grew rapidly, debates over creating professional municipal police forces gained urgency—paralleling similar discussions in Britain and Europe.

In this chapter, we will explore:

1. **Colonial Roots**: Transplanting English sheriff and constable models to the New World, plus the role of militias in frontier communities.
2. **Slave Patrols** in the American South, where policing was intricately linked to maintaining an enslaved labor force.
3. **Night Watch and Volunteer Systems** in early American cities, their strengths and weaknesses, and the push for more professional approaches.
4. **Post-Revolutionary Developments**: How independence affected policing structures, balancing local autonomy with calls for stronger central authority in certain contexts.
5. **The Rise of Urban Police** during the first half of the 19th century, culminating in the establishment of forces in major cities and the influence of reform-minded officials.
6. **Regional Variations**—the Northeast's urban centers, the agrarian South, and the rapidly expanding Western frontier—and how these contexts produced differing policing methods.

We will conclude by positioning early American policing alongside the broader global transformations we have already seen, setting the stage for more cohesive and professional forces by the mid- to late 19th century.

1. Colonial Law Enforcement: The English Legacy

1.1. Sheriffs, Constables, and the Watch

When English settlers founded colonies in North America (early 17th century onward), they brought familiar law enforcement offices:

- **Sheriff**: Typically appointed by colonial governors, charged with tax collection, executing writs, and managing local jails. Sheriffs were powerful but spread thin in rural counties.
- **Constable**: A local figure, often selected by townspeople or the court, to handle minor offenses, serve warrants, and oversee the watch. This was usually a part-time role with limited authority.
- **Night Watch**: Volunteers or conscripts patrolled streets after dark, raising the "hue and cry" if they witnessed wrongdoing. These watchmen were famously under-trained and sometimes drowsy on duty.

Though these practices mirrored traditional English methods, the vast distances and smaller populations in the colonies shaped their application. Sparse settlements meant that a single sheriff might cover an enormous county, relying on informal posses when needed. Meanwhile, towns in New England combined religious and communal norms with constables and watch duties, fostering a sense of collective responsibility for order.

1.2. Variations by Region

Colonial America was not uniform:

- **New England**: Smaller towns, tight-knit communities, and Puritan moral codes. Local watch systems often doubled as moral guardians, punishing public drunkenness or Sabbath-breaking.
- **Middle Colonies**: Ethnically diverse, with larger port cities like Philadelphia or New York. Policing these growing urban centers was more complex, leading to more formal night watches.
- **Southern Colonies**: Landed gentry and plantation economies, with large rural districts. Sheriffs had broad authority, but daily patrolling was minimal outside plantation areas—aside from **slave patrols**.

Despite regional differences, a shared reliance on part-time watchmen, unpaid constables, and informal militias characterized colonial policing. Full-time, professional police did not yet exist.

2. Slave Patrols in the American South

2.1. Origins and Purpose

From the 17th to the mid-19th centuries, slavery expanded dramatically in the Southern colonies/states. Enslaved Africans formed a large labor force on plantations. To maintain control over this population and deter rebellions:

- **Slave Codes**: Laws that restricted the movement and activities of enslaved people, requiring passes to travel, forbidding literacy, and imposing harsh punishments for insurrection.
- **Patrols**: Organized groups of white men who rode through rural areas, stopping suspected runaways, checking passes, and searching slave quarters for weapons or contraband.

2.2. Structure and Enforcement

Slave patrols were often mandated by colonial or state statutes:

- **Community Obligation**: White men (especially non-elite) were required to serve in patrols on a rotating basis. This spread the burden of policing enslaved people across the white population, reinforcing racial hierarchy.
- **Violent Tactics**: Patrols carried whips and guns, using intimidation and force to maintain subjugation. Any sign of resistance or insubordination could lead to brutal reprisals.

- **Collaboration with Sheriffs**: If a runaway slave was captured, patrols brought them to the sheriff's custody for punishment or return to the owner.

These patrols form a key chapter in the history of policing in America, distinctly tying law enforcement to the preservation of slavery and racial control. Even after the American Revolution championed liberty, Southern states clung to slave patrols until the Civil War (1861–1865).

2.3. Long-Term Impact

Though the direct institution of slave patrols ended with the Civil War's conclusion and the abolition of slavery, their legacy influenced post-war policing, especially in the Reconstruction and Jim Crow eras (beyond our current scope). It highlights how American policing in some regions was shaped not just by European traditions, but by the demands of an economy and social system built on enslaved labor.

3. The Night Watch and Volunteer System in Early American Cities

3.1. Growth of Urban Centers

By the late 18th and early 19th centuries, ports like **Boston**, **New York**, **Philadelphia**, **Baltimore**, and **Charleston** saw population surges:

- **Trade Hubs**: Ships arrived from Europe, the Caribbean, and beyond, bringing goods and immigrants.
- **Dense Neighborhoods**: Overcrowded housing, taverns, and alleyways created new opportunities for theft and violence.
- **Firefighting and Public Health**: Urban governance also worried about fires, epidemics, and sanitation, sometimes assigning watchmen these additional duties.

3.2. Limitations of Volunteer Patrols

Typically, watchmen were either volunteers or poorly paid, drawn from the local community:

- **Irregular Attendance**: Many watchmen had day jobs and dreaded late-night shifts. Some were elderly or unfit, while others slept on the job or accepted bribes to ignore certain crimes.
- **Corruption and Nepotism**: Local politicians might staff the watch with loyal supporters, diminishing professionalism.
- **Reactive Policing**: The watch mostly responded to immediate disturbances. Preventive patrol was minimal, and investigative capacity was negligible.

3.3. Calls for Reform

Wealthy merchants and emerging middle classes increasingly demanded more consistent policing. As burglary, public drunkenness, and street gangs seemed to rise, critics argued that volunteer systems no longer sufficed. Newspapers reported sensational crimes, fueling panic and pressuring city councils to consider organized, salaried officers. This foreshadowed major reforms in the mid-19th century, but the momentum began in these earlier decades.

4. Post-Revolutionary Impact on Policing Structures

4.1. Changing Political Context

After the **American Revolution** (1775–1783), states wrote constitutions that emphasized citizens' rights, local governance, and a distrust of standing armies (including, by extension, heavily armed national police). Key influences included:

- **Individual Liberties**: Founding documents stressed personal freedoms, shaping attitudes that policing should remain local, limited, and closely watched by the populace.
- **State vs. Federal Authority**: Policing typically stayed under state or municipal jurisdiction. The federal government had minimal direct role in everyday law enforcement, aside from customs officers or marshals for federal courts.
- **Community Traditions**: Many Americans continued to prefer the idea of local self-help and the posse comitatus principle (citizens mobilized by a sheriff) rather than a professional police force, which smacked of British "tyranny."

4.2. Institutional Developments

Still, the new republic did see some changes:

- **Marshals and District Courts**: The Judiciary Act of 1789 established a system of federal courts and the office of U.S. Marshals to execute federal laws, deliver court papers, and handle prisoners. Marshals sometimes recruited local men for enforcement tasks.
- **Militia Acts**: Organized militias could be called upon for large-scale crises. In practice, these militias combined civil and military functions, bridging the gap between a standing army and local watch.
- **Urban Experimentation**: Major cities began to pass ordinances to formalize the night watch, improve watchmen's pay, or create inspector roles for certain offenses (e.g., health inspectors, fire inspectors, or market inspectors).

These modest expansions of law enforcement revealed a gradual shift from purely volunteer or amateur systems toward more formal, if still localized, agencies.

5. The Rise of Municipal Police in the Early 19th Century

5.1. Population Boom and Public Disorder

Between 1800 and 1850, the U.S. population grew rapidly, fueled by immigration and westward migration. Cities struggled with:

- **Overcrowded Tenements**: Particularly in coastal hubs like New York, immigrants crammed into slums with unsanitary conditions.
- **Ethnic Tensions**: Rivalries between different immigrant groups (Irish, German, etc.) sometimes erupted into street fights or riots.
- **Economic Inequality**: A new working class confronted exploitative labor conditions, occasionally leading to strikes or unrest.

Existing watch systems seemed overwhelmed. Riots and large-scale disturbances—like the **1835 Great Fire of New York** (which also involved looting) or the **1844 Philadelphia nativist riots**—underscored the need for a more robust policing approach.

5.2. Early Police Forces in Major Cities

Inspired partly by public demands and the example of London's Metropolitan Police (founded 1829), some U.S. cities experimented with professional forces:

- **New York**: In 1844, state legislation combined day and night watches into a unified police department. Officers were paid, wore distinctive badges (though full uniforms came later), and patrolled assigned "beats" more systematically.
- **Boston**: Established a formal police department in 1838, initially focusing on merchant districts to deter theft, eventually expanding citywide.
- **Philadelphia**: Created a full-time police force in the 1850s after repeated riots showed the volunteer watch's ineffectiveness.

These early departments faced skepticism—some believed a standing city police might become an "urban army" violating civil liberties. But business owners, property holders, and middle-class reformers often supported the transition.

5.3. Policing Philosophies

Debates raged about how American police should act:

- **Preventive Patrol**: Borrowing from Peel's principles, city forces deployed officers on regular foot patrol to discourage crime by their visible presence.
- **Accountability**: Elected officials or city councils typically oversaw police budgets, appointments, and discipline. This occasionally led to political patronage and corruption, yet it also gave local communities a voice in policing.
- **Use of Force**: Policemen in the 19th century carried clubs and sometimes firearms. Public concern about excessive force shaped departmental rules, but standards varied widely from one city to another.

By the mid-19th century, a distinctly American model of municipal policing emerged: local government control, full-time salaries, foot patrols, and close ties to urban political machines (e.g., Tammany Hall in New York). This system was still evolving as industrialization and immigration continued to transform American cities.

6. Regional Differences: North, South, and the Frontier

6.1. The Northern and Eastern States

As noted, the Northeast led the way in forming municipal police departments, driven by dense urban populations. They faced challenges like:

- **Ethnic Riots**: Boston and New York saw conflicts between Irish Catholic immigrants and nativist groups. Police had to manage sectarian tensions and election-related violence.
- **Labor Unrest**: The beginnings of organized labor in the 1830s–1840s forced police to confront strikers and protests, sometimes with bias in favor of business owners.

6.2. The South

In the southern states, policing retained distinctive features:

- **Slave Patrol Continuation**: Until the Civil War, rural counties and towns depended on these patrols to control enslaved people. City police forces also emerged in southern ports (e.g., Charleston, Savannah, New Orleans), but their duties included watching for runaway slaves or suppressing gatherings of free people of color.
- **Post-Emancipation Tensions**: The formal end of slave patrols lies outside our timeframe, yet the antebellum policing tradition heavily influenced how law enforcement functioned in the region—focusing on controlling the Black population and protecting planter interests.

6.3. The Western Frontier

As settlers pushed west, new territories adopted a mix of volunteer posses, vigilante committees, and elected sheriffs:

- **Sparse Populations**: Small, scattered towns lacked funds for full-time police. Sheriffs, marshals, or local committees handled law enforcement, sometimes resorting to extrajudicial actions (e.g., frontier justice or lynchings) due to weak court systems.
- **Mining Camps and Cattle Towns**: Boomtowns near gold or silver strikes, or cattle trails, faced waves of transient workers, gamblers, and criminals.

Hastily formed "miners' courts" or vigilante groups policed these rough communities.
- **Federal Marshals**: In territories awaiting statehood, U.S. Marshals and deputy marshals served as a backbone for federal legal authority, especially near major routes or sites of federal interest.

This diversity in the West underscores how local conditions (mineral rushes, ranching, tribal conflicts) produced policing solutions that varied widely from the formal city forces in the East.

7. The Role of Technology and Communication

7.1. Telegraph and Railroad

Although still in its infancy in the early 19th century, the **telegraph** (commercially introduced in the 1840s) and expanding **railroads** began to influence policing:

- **Faster Warrant Transmission**: Sheriffs or city police could receive instructions or alerts from distant cities more quickly, improving interstate pursuit of criminals.
- **Railroad Police**: Private railroad companies hired their own security agents to protect cargo and stations, forming a quasi-private policing system that sometimes overlapped with public authorities.

7.2. Firearms

American frontier culture and the Second Amendment tradition meant that many citizens owned firearms. Policemen, especially in cities, sometimes carried guns by the mid-19th century, though policies varied. This contrasted with the early British police, who initially avoided firearms to maintain a non-military appearance.

8. Mid-19th Century Trends and Looking Ahead

By the 1850s, several American cities had established professional police departments, bringing:

- **Regular Patrols**: Officers assigned to "beats" or districts they walked daily.

- **Organizational Hierarchies**: Police chiefs, captains, and sergeants gave order to the force.
- **Corruption and Patronage**: Urban political machines often used police jobs as rewards for loyal supporters, leading to bribery and selective law enforcement.

Public debates continued about how to fund police, hold them accountable, and balance their power with citizen rights. Meanwhile, the **Civil War** (1861-1865) was on the horizon, which would transform law enforcement in the South and prompt new federal interventions.

9. Parallels and Contrasts with Europe and Beyond

9.1. Similarities

In broad terms, early American policing shared key traits with Europe:

- **Gradual Professionalization**: Volunteer or part-time watches gave way to salaried forces.
- **Urban Focus**: The impetus for reform often came from crowded cities worried about crime, riots, and civil disorder.
- **Political Oversight**: City governments, not centralized national agencies, typically directed the police—similar to many continental European states that balanced local autonomy with state guidance.

9.2. Differences

However, the U.S. context had unique elements:

- **Slave Patrol Legacy**: Tying law enforcement to race-based oppression in the South left a deep imprint absent in most European policing traditions.
- **Frontier Vigilantism**: The lack of strong state structures in newly settled territories encouraged extralegal "justice," a phenomenon less common in Europe by the 19th century.
- **Less Direct Influence of a National Government**: Until well after the Civil War, the federal role in policing was minimal, contrasting with certain European countries' centralized models (like France's Ministry of Police or Prussia's strong gendarmerie).

Chapter 15

Impact of the Industrial Revolution on Policing

The Industrial Revolution, which began in Britain in the late 18th century and spread across much of Europe and parts of North America in the 19th century, ushered in profound changes in society, economy, and everyday life. Factories rose in once-rural landscapes, urban populations soared, and new social classes—industrial workers and a burgeoning middle class—transformed the dynamics of labor and capital. These sweeping developments had a direct and far-reaching impact on how societies thought about and implemented policing.

In this chapter, we will explore:

1. **How industrialization spurred rapid urban growth**, creating crowded cities that demanded new policing solutions.
2. **Social upheaval and new forms of crime**, including labor riots, theft on a larger scale, and the presence of transient workers.
3. **Philosophical shifts in governance**, as states grappled with the challenge of maintaining order without stifling the economic dynamism of the times.
4. **Technology and communication advances** that shaped policing responses, from improved transport to better administrative record-keeping.
5. **The spread of formal police forces** influenced by Britain's example and the ongoing need for systematic, proactive law enforcement in industrial settings.
6. **Differences in approach** among nations that industrialized at various speeds, with some places embracing modern policing while others hesitated due to political or cultural reservations.

By examining these themes, we will see how the Industrial Revolution not only accelerated economic development but also propelled major reforms in policing structures, philosophies, and day-to-day practices throughout much of the world in the mid to late 19th century.

1. The Rise of Industrial Cities

1.1. Population Booms

Before the Industrial Revolution, most people in Europe and North America lived in rural villages or small towns. With the expansion of factories and mills in places like Manchester, Liverpool, and Birmingham in Britain, or Lowell in the United States, populations rapidly shifted. By the early to mid-19th century:

- **Manchester**: Once a modest market town, it ballooned into a sprawling industrial center. This swift increase in population overwhelmed traditional volunteer watch systems and created greater anonymity among residents.
- **New Urban Layouts**: Neighborhoods of cramped, hastily built housing sprang up around factories. Narrow, unlit alleys and poorly maintained streets provided cover for thieves and aggravated public health concerns.

Governments soon realized that older rural policing methods—like occasional night watches or part-time constables—could not cope with these dense, fast-growing populations. Crime patterns changed, and so did public expectations about safety.

1.2. Diverse Populations and Transient Workers

Industrial cities attracted migrants from the countryside and, increasingly, from other countries. This rapid influx meant:

- **Language and Cultural Barriers**: Police had to navigate neighborhoods where residents spoke different dialects or languages. Communication challenges complicated investigations and patrols.
- **Transient Labor**: Factories hired workers on short-term or seasonal contracts. Many laborers shared cramped lodging, then moved on if they lost their jobs or sought better wages elsewhere. This mobility made it harder to track suspects or build stable community relationships.
- **Social Strain**: Tensions flared between long-established urban dwellers and newcomers. Sometimes, local watch or incipient police forces were caught in the middle of ethnic clashes, strikes, or mass protests.

Where older watch systems relied on everyone knowing each other, the anonymity of industrial towns eroded that model. Policing had to adjust to more impersonal, larger-scale conditions.

2. New Forms of Crime and Social Conflict

2.1. Urban Crime Waves

Though the notion of a "crime wave" was often tied to moral panic, actual changes in crime did occur:

- **Pickpocketing and Mugging**: Crowded streets, markets, and factory gates offered opportunities for thieves to operate quickly and vanish into the throngs.
- **Burglary**: Poorly lit back alleys and flimsy housing made breaking and entering easier. Some gangs specialized in stealing from factory yards or shipping depots at night.
- **Prostitution and Vices**: The growth of red-light districts in industrial cities led to heightened concerns about public morals. Many moral reformers demanded that police crack down on these "dens of iniquity."

Unlike earlier rural societies—where local watchers might know all the townsfolk—industrial cities housed strangers living side by side. Criminal networks found it simpler to hide among the masses. Consequently, calls for a more systematic, professional police presence grew louder.

2.2. Labor Riots and Strikes

Industrialization also brought labor unrest:

- **Poor Working Conditions**: Long hours, minimal pay, and unsafe machinery fueled worker discontent. Groups of laborers banded together, staging strikes or machine-smashing actions (like the Luddites in early 19th-century Britain).
- **Police and Militia Involvement**: When protests turned into riots, local authorities might call the military or newly formed police to restore order. The violent suppression of strikers, however, risked stoking further grievances.
- **Moral and Political Debates**: Governments teetered between sympathizing with industrial growth (and thus owners' needs) and recognizing that mass labor protests could destabilize society. Policing became a tool to mediate, or forcibly quell, these conflicts.

Riots around wage cuts, factory closures, or harsh working environments were common in booming industrial hubs, placing unique pressure on evolving police organizations to handle large crowds, protect property, and manage public fear.

2.3. Class Tensions

Victorian-era Britain (and much of Europe) saw intensifying class distinctions, with a clear divide between wealthy industrialists and working-class laborers:

- **Middle-Class Fears**: Property owners worried about thieves, vagrants, and the potential for revolutionary zeal among impoverished workers. Many supported stronger police measures as a safeguard.
- **Policing as Class Control**: Critics argued that new police forces existed primarily to protect middle- and upper-class interests—factories, shops, and private dwellings—rather than to serve the poor.
- **Demand for Fairness**: Some reformers insisted that police should defend the "public peace" impartially, applying laws equally across all classes. The notion of policing "by consent," championed by Sir Robert Peel in Britain, reflected this ideal—though practice varied significantly.

Amid these tensions, the Industrial Revolution spurred both a fear of disorder and a recognition that robust, well-organized policing might help maintain civil society.

3. Philosophical and Governance Shifts

3.1. Liberal and Utilitarian Influences

In the early to mid-19th century, liberal thinkers, as well as utilitarian philosophers like Jeremy Bentham, argued for rational, standardized governance:

- **Systematic Administration**: They believed a strong but fair state apparatus could optimize societal well-being. Policing became a key component in ensuring safety and predictability for commerce and personal life.
- **Preventive Policing**: Building on Enlightenment and Napoleonic ideas, the concept of preventing crime, rather than merely reacting to it, gained acceptance. Sufficient patrolling and timely interventions were seen as more humane and efficient than relying on draconian punishments post-crime.
- **Legal Codification**: Countries such as France (with the Napoleonic Code) and states within the German Confederation introduced clearer penal codes. These developments made it easier for police to understand and enforce laws uniformly.

3.2. The Role of the Central State

Pre-industrial policing often relied on local authority—villages, towns, or feudal lords. With growing national bureaucracies in the 19th century:

- **Government Oversight**: Monarchies or parliaments established ministries of the interior or police, standardizing practices.
- **National Pride and Legitimacy**: A well-ordered society became a marker of modern progress. Rival states observed each other's successes, sometimes adopting or adapting foreign policing innovations.
- **Resistance to Central Control**: Some regions, especially in newly formed nation-states like Italy or Germany, resisted top-down authority. Local elites or communities feared losing autonomy. The industrial era pushed states to unify policing, but not without friction.

These philosophical and administrative underpinnings contributed to the professionalization of police forces, solidifying them as pillars of the emerging industrial nations.

4. Technology and Communication Advances

4.1. Railways and Telegraph

Industrial-era transportation and communication breakthroughs had a direct influence on law enforcement:

- **Rail Networks**: The ability to travel quickly across regions meant criminals could escape more easily, but it also allowed police to pursue suspects or coordinate cross-jurisdictional efforts.
- **Telegraph Lines**: By mid-19th century, police in some areas could transmit urgent messages to distant stations, streamlining the search for fugitives or runaways.
- **Passport Controls**: As governments took advantage of faster communication, they sometimes tightened internal passport requirements (in continental Europe) to track and monitor movement of suspicious individuals.

4.2. Record-Keeping and Forensic Beginnings

While modern forensics were still in their infancy, the industrial period saw improvements in bureaucracy:

- **Centralized Criminal Registers**: Authorities began compiling lists of known offenders, shared across multiple towns or regions.
- **Photographic Technology**: By the 1840s and 1850s, early photography emerged. Although not immediately widespread, it hinted at future police use for mug shots and crime scene documentation.
- **Physical Evidence**: Some larger city forces experimented with better evidence gathering—recording footprints, collecting personal items left at scenes, etc. These steps were rudimentary but foreshadowed the rise of detective work later in the century.

These technological developments allowed a more coordinated policing environment, aligning with the demands of an increasingly interconnected industrial society.

5. Spread of Formal Police Forces

5.1. Britain's Influence

Britain, the cradle of the Industrial Revolution, spearheaded systematic policing reforms. The London Metropolitan Police (founded 1829) became a reference point:

- **Expansion to Other Cities**: Industrial centers like Manchester, Birmingham, and Leeds followed London's model, creating professional forces with full-time officers on the beat.
- **County and Rural Policing**: By the mid-19th century, legislation (e.g., the County Police Acts) encouraged or mandated professional policing across rural areas too, spurred by fears of traveling criminals and farm theft.

5.2. Continental Europe

Countries like France, Belgium, the German states, and the Austro-Hungarian Empire also recognized the need for robust police:

- **Napoleonic Legacy**: France, under successive regimes, maintained a national gendarmerie and urban police forces. Industrial hubs such as Lyon or Lille adopted more uniform patrols.
- **German Principalities**: States like Prussia had a tradition of centralized bureaucracy. As they industrialized, they expanded municipal forces in Berlin, Hamburg, and other cities, melding military discipline with Peel-style policing theories.
- **Austria-Hungary**: Vienna's police gradually modernized, though bureaucratic complexities across various ethnic regions made uniform standards challenging.

Across these regions, industrial growth fueled the belief that professional, state-backed police were essential for public order, commercial security, and, in many cases, the control of political dissent.

5.3. The United States

As discussed in Chapter 14, the U.S. also felt industrial pressures:

- **Northern Cities**: Places like New York, Boston, and Philadelphia began professionalizing forces by the 1840s–1850s. Immigration surges (Irish, German, etc.) and crowded tenements heightened the perceived need for regular patrols.
- **Differences from Europe**: Many American police remained under local political control, with less direct national oversight. While they shared Europe's impetus for controlling crime in industrial settings, the U.S. context also involved racial tensions and frontier expansions.

Thus, by the mid-19th century, the concept of a recognizable, uniformed police officer patrolling industrial streets was fast becoming the norm in major cities across industrializing nations.

6. Challenges and Criticisms

6.1. Corruption and Political Influence

Even as new police forces emerged, many struggled with graft or undue influence:

- **Urban Political Machines**: In places like the U.S. (e.g., Tammany Hall in New York) or municipal councils in Europe, local politicians doled out police jobs or promotions to loyal supporters.
- **Bribery and Patronage**: Some police officers accepted payments from brothel owners, gambling rings, or factory bosses who sought leniency. This undermined public trust and triggered repeated reform efforts.
- **Anti-Police Sentiment**: Working-class communities often saw police as tools of the wealthy. Clashes during strikes or protests fueled accusations of bias in law enforcement.

6.2. Brutality and Overreach

With the advent of more organized forces, concerns about excessive force grew:

- **Riot Policing**: Early police lacked specialized training for crowd control. Violent dispersals of labor demonstrations sometimes resulted in deaths, stoking resentment.
- **Authoritarian Tactics**: States with absolute or semi-absolute rulers (e.g., parts of central Europe) used police to crush political dissent. Secret

policing and censorship created fear, reminiscent of Napoleonic practices.
- **Public Outcry**: Journalists and reformers demanded accountability, advocating for rules on the use of force and legal constraints on arrests.

6.3. Unequal Enforcement

Industrial societies were rife with inequality:

- **Slum Districts**: Police presence could be more frequent and harsher in impoverished neighborhoods, leading to tension with the urban poor.
- **Ethnic Minorities**: Immigrant enclaves often complained of discriminatory policing. Language barriers or cultural biases intensified misunderstandings.
- **Factory Owners' Influence**: In many industrial towns, local elites funded police expansions, expecting them to protect property above all else. Some forces prioritized factory and shop security over concerns of working-class communities.

These criticisms did not stop the growth of formal police institutions but fueled ongoing debates about reform, fairness, and the role of policing in an industrial democracy.

7. Evolving Police Roles and Specializations

7.1. The Birth of Detective Work

Mid-19th century industrial settings led to complex crimes—organized burglary rings, financial fraud, and cross-regional criminal networks. Police departments began creating detective branches:

- **London's Detective Branch (1842)**: The Metropolitan Police formed a small group of investigators specializing in major crimes.
- **Paris Sûreté**: Building on a tradition that stretched back to the early 19th century (under Eugène François Vidocq), Parisian detectives tracked criminals across departmental lines.
- **Expanding Techniques**: Detectives used informants, surveillance, and early record-keeping of known offenders. While forensics remained rudimentary, detective units symbolized a shift toward proactive, intelligence-led policing.

7.2. Police in Public Health and Safety

Industrial cities dealt with cholera outbreaks, contaminated water supplies, and cramped housing. Some police forces took on broader civic duties:

- **Fire Inspections**: Checking for fire hazards in factories or crowded tenements.
- **Health Regulations**: Enforcing quarantine or public health orders during epidemics.
- **Urban Planning**: Helping manage street lighting, signage, and traffic flow for horse-drawn vehicles.

Though these roles varied by city and country, many recognized that a stable, healthy urban environment supported both economic prosperity and social order.

7.3. Moral Regulation

During the Victorian era, moral campaigns targeted prostitution, gambling, and alcohol abuse:

- **Public House Regulations**: Police might monitor taverns to enforce closing times or license restrictions.
- **Vice Squads**: In some larger forces, specialized officers focused on brothels or gambling dens, reflecting middle-class pressure to "clean up" cities.

- **Critiques of Overreach**: Critics warned that policing morality risked infringing on personal freedoms, sparking debates about the proper scope of state intervention.

These expansions of police responsibility underscored how the industrial era transformed the traditional watchman into a more multifaceted agent of public authority.

8. The Global Impact of Industrial Policing

8.1. Colonial Contexts

As industrial powers expanded overseas, they carried their policing models into colonies:

- **India** (under British rule): After the Indian Rebellion of 1857, the British reorganized policing, creating a more centralized force. They aimed to control large populations, quell rebellions, and protect commercial interests (railways, ports, etc.).
- **Africa**: In newly claimed territories, European colonial administrations formed paramilitary police or constabularies to enforce tax collection, maintain labor control, and suppress local resistance.
- **Southeast Asia**: French Indochina or the Dutch East Indies imported systems that blended metropolitan practices with local enforcers. These forces often focused on ensuring order beneficial to the colonial economy.

Industrialization in the metropole influenced how colonial rulers viewed policing: as a tool not just for crime control but also for consolidating imperial authority over vast, culturally diverse subjects.

8.2. Information Exchange

Global trade and communication allowed countries to observe each other's policing successes and failures:

- **Policing Conferences**: By the late 19th century, informal exchanges of ideas began among European officials, hinting at early international cooperation (though formal bodies like Interpol would appear later, in the 20th century).

- **Migration of Officers**: Some retired British or French officers served as advisors in other states. Japan, for example, studied European police models during the Meiji era.
- **Adaptations to Local Realities**: Even where foreign advisors introduced new policing methods, local traditions, legal systems, and power structures inevitably shaped the final result.

Industrial-era policing, thus, was not confined to Europe or North America; it influenced and was influenced by global interactions.

9. Seeds of Future Reform

9.1. Early Calls for Professional Standards

By the late 19th century, critics recognized persistent issues: corruption, brutality, and inefficiency. Reformers proposed:

- **Merit-Based Recruitment**: Rather than letting politics decide appointments, they advocated competitive exams or training schools.
- **Clear Disciplinary Codes**: Internal rules for officer conduct and a more transparent complaint process.
- **Integration of Forensic Science**: While still young, the promise of fingerprinting, photography, and systematic evidence collection loomed on the horizon, offering more scientific policing.

9.2. Social Reform Movements

Labor activists, socialists, and early social reformers saw police as integral to shaping the industrial city:

- **Better Working Conditions**: Reformers argued that policing alone could not solve crime if poverty and unemployment went unaddressed.
- **Public Safety vs. Political Control**: Groups demanded that police focus on genuine crime reduction, not political repression of union meetings or socialist gatherings.
- **Urban Planning**: Advocates believed improved housing, sanitation, and education would reduce crime more effectively than an ever-expanding police force.

Chapter 16

Victorian-Era Police Reforms

The Victorian era, spanning the reign of Queen Victoria in Britain from 1837 to 1901, coincided with a period of intense social and economic change that extended well beyond the British Isles. It was an age of expanding empires, rapid industrialization, and growing public consciousness about crime, morality, and governance. During these decades, police forces became more established, less controversial in some circles, and subject to an array of reforms that refined their structure, mission, and public relations.

While the term "Victorian" is specifically British, the trends in policing from roughly the 1840s to the early 1900s resonated throughout Europe, North America, and beyond. Many countries faced similar questions: How could the police best handle urban crowds, moral offenses, and more complex crimes? How should officers be trained and supervised to ensure professionalism? What boundaries should exist between the police and political authorities?

In this chapter, we will examine:

1. **The consolidation of professional police** in Britain, including regional expansion and the enshrinement of Peel's principles.
2. **Efforts to address police corruption**, ensure accountability, and institute training programs.
3. **Moral campaigns** that placed police at the forefront of vice suppression, social hygiene, and public decency regulations.
4. **The rise of detective work** and the formation of specialized investigation units, culminating in high-profile cases that shaped public expectations.
5. **Public perception** of the police, from acceptance and respect to suspicion and criticism, especially concerning class bias and heavy-handed tactics.
6. **International parallels**, as other nations observed and adapted Victorian-era reforms to their own policing contexts.

By understanding Victorian-era reforms, we gain insight into how policing evolved from a fledgling, often-questioned institution into a more accepted civic body—though certainly not without ongoing debate over its powers and priorities.

1. Consolidation of Police Forces in Britain

1.1. Growth After the Metropolitan Model

Following Sir Robert Peel's introduction of the Metropolitan Police in 1829, the subsequent decades solidified the concept of professional policing across Britain:

- **Municipal Corporations Act (1835)**: Gave borough councils more authority to set up or revamp local police. Many towns followed London's example, adopting uniformed, full-time patrols.
- **County Police Acts (1839, 1840, 1856)**: Gradually extended professional forces into rural areas. By the mid-1850s, most counties established official police, though some resisted on cost or principle grounds.
- **Scotland and Ireland**: Separate but parallel developments occurred, with the City of Glasgow Police recognized as one of the earliest professional forces (founded 1800). Ireland's policing model differed due to political tensions, culminating in the Royal Irish Constabulary, a more militarized body.

By mid-century, the notion of the "bobby on the beat"—an approachable officer patrolling the streets—had become a standard fixture in towns and cities across Britain.

1.2. Central Oversight and Funding

A key Victorian development was increased **state oversight** of local forces:

- **Home Office Influence**: Though many forces were locally managed, the Home Office in London offered grants and set guidelines, expecting forces to meet certain standards.
- **National Inspectors**: Inspectors from central government periodically reviewed local constabularies to assess efficiency, discipline, and record-keeping. Forces that failed to meet criteria risked losing government subsidies.
- **Uniform Standards**: The desire for consistent training and equipment across counties shaped the creation of manuals for police procedures and conduct.

This mild centralization balanced local accountability with the perceived benefits of national coordination, ensuring that British policing as a whole moved in a broadly unified direction.

2. Police Corruption and Reforms

2.1. Early Scandals

As forces expanded, so did opportunities for corruption:

- **Bribery and Collusion**: Some officers took payoffs from illegal gambling houses or unlicensed pubs to turn a blind eye.
- **Nepotism**: In small towns, police appointments sometimes went to friends or relatives of local councillors, undermining merit-based recruitment.
- **Public Trials and Press**: Victorian newspapers exposed scandals, stirring public debate and prompting official inquiries.

2.2. Professionalization Measures

Reformers and senior officers responded with initiatives aimed at professional integrity:

- **Disciplinary Regulations**: Codes of conduct spelled out acceptable behavior, with punishments for misconduct ranging from fines to dismissal.
- **Recruitment Standards**: Physical fitness requirements, minimum literacy levels, and moral character checks became more common.
- **Training Depots**: London's Metropolitan Police established training depots where recruits learned basic law, patrolling tactics, and record-keeping. Other cities followed suit, gradually phasing out the older, ad-hoc orientation.

This emphasis on discipline and standardized procedures increased public confidence, even if problems persisted. The Victorian period saw policing as a potential career path rather than a last-resort job.

2.3. Emergence of Internal Oversight

In larger forces, internal oversight units began to appear:

- **Inspection and Audit**: Senior officers audited station logbooks, expense accounts, and complaint records to spot patterns of wrongdoing or negligence.
- **Periodic Restructuring**: Some major cities reorganized their police command structures, adding layers of supervision (chief constables, superintendents, inspectors) to ensure accountability.
- **Civilian Complaint Input** (Limited): While formal complaint boards were rare, city councils or watch committees often fielded grievances from residents, occasionally investigating them.

These changes laid the groundwork for more formalized mechanisms of police accountability that would evolve in the 20th century.

3. Moral Campaigns and Policing

3.1. The Victorian Moral Climate

The Victorian era was marked by strong beliefs in respectability, self-control, and social propriety:

- **Temperance Movement**: Advocates pushed to reduce alcohol consumption, seeing drunkenness as a root of crime. Police were expected to enforce licensing laws and curtail rowdy tavern behavior.
- **Prostitution**: Reformers labeled prostitutes as "fallen women" who threatened society's moral fabric. Laws like the Contagious Diseases Acts (1860s) gave police new authority to arrest women suspected of prostitution near military towns, though these acts were deeply controversial.
- **Gambling and Vices**: Middle-class pressure groups demanded crackdowns on illicit gambling dens, betting houses, and similar "sinful" activities.

3.2. Police Role in Social Regulation

Local police forces found themselves at the forefront of moral regulation:

- **Raids on Brothels**: Under public pressure, police conducted periodic sweeps of suspected brothels or "immoral houses," often guided by local moral societies' tip-offs.
- **Enforcing Sunday Laws**: Many communities had rules against Sunday trading, leisure activities, or public entertainments. Police might be tasked with shutting down shops or removing peddlers.
- **Street Cleanliness**: Police sometimes oversaw aspects of sanitation or street order, removing beggars, street performers, or petty hawkers deemed nuisances.

3.3. Critiques of Overreach

Not everyone approved of police involvement in private morals:

- **Civil Liberties Concerns**: Radicals, some liberals, and working-class voices argued that policing personal behavior invaded personal freedoms.
- **Selective Enforcement**: Critics noted that wealthy patrons of clandestine clubs rarely faced the same scrutiny as poor or immigrant neighborhoods suspected of vice.
- **Gender Debates**: The Contagious Diseases Acts stirred women's rights activists like Josephine Butler, who condemned the police power to forcibly examine females suspected of prostitution. Their campaigns eventually led to the Acts' repeal.

This mix of moral fervor and pushback shaped the Victorian police mission, often straddling the line between public order and private intrusion.

4. The Rise of Detective Policing

4.1. Creating Detective Branches

While uniformed "beat" policing garnered most attention in the early Victorian era, the mid- to late 19th century saw detective work flourish:

- **Detective Branch of the Met Police (1842)**: London established a small team of plainclothes officers focusing on serious crimes—burglaries, murders, forgeries. Over time, this grew into the Criminal Investigation Department (CID) in 1878.
- **Regional Cities**: Glasgow, Liverpool, and other major cities formed detective squads, often learning from London's experiences.

- **European Counterparts**: Paris had its Sûreté, Berlin and Vienna also instituted detective units, reflecting a Europe-wide trend of specialized investigation.

4.2. High-Profile Cases

Sensational investigations captured public imagination:

- **Jack the Ripper (1888)**: The Metropolitan Police's attempts to catch the infamous killer in London's Whitechapel district showcased both the potentials and limitations of Victorian detective methods. The case highlighted the need for better forensic techniques, communication, and public cooperation.
- **Forgery and White-Collar Crimes**: Detectives pursued fraudsters exploiting new financial systems (e.g., banknotes, checks). Skilled detective work often prevented large-scale monetary losses, boosting the profession's prestige.
- **Notorious Murder Trials**: The press avidly covered detective-led investigations, shaping a "celebrity detective" archetype (e.g., Inspector Frederick Abberline or, in fiction, Sherlock Holmes by Arthur Conan Doyle).

Such cases made detective policing a fixture in newspapers and popular culture, elevating the detective's role as a crime-fighting hero while also exposing flaws in existing techniques.

4.3. Forensic Progress

While still rudimentary by modern standards, late Victorian policing adopted early forensic notions:

- **Photography**: Police began taking mug shots of suspects. Some forces photographed crime scenes or corpses to preserve evidence.
- **Anthropometry**: Inspired by Alphonse Bertillon's system in France, some British forces measured suspects' body dimensions to identify repeat offenders. Fingerprinting, introduced in British India in the 1850s for administrative tasks, would later make its way into detective policing near the century's end.
- **Record Keeping**: Organized files on criminals, modus operandi, and addresses improved as station clerks used systematic methods. National

or regional bulletins circulated descriptions of wanted persons, bridging earlier communication gaps.

Though these developments were modest steps, they set the stage for the more scientific policing breakthroughs of the early 20th century.

5. Public Perception and Class Bias

5.1. Growing Acceptance

By the mid-Victorian era, many middle-class and some working-class citizens came to see the police as a stabilizing force:

- **Reduction in Street Crime**: Visible patrols discouraged opportunistic theft, bringing a sense of relative safety to commercial districts.
- **Fire and Accident Assistance**: In some towns, police also helped with firefighting or rescue operations, fostering goodwill.
- **Charitable Ventures**: Police sometimes participated in philanthropic events, further softening their image as purely repressive agents.

5.2. Continuing Distrust

Not all segments welcomed the police:

- **Working-Class Neighborhoods**: Some residents perceived police as siding with factory owners or landlords, especially during strikes or evictions. Tensions flared when mass arrests occurred at labor protests.
- **Political Radicals**: Socialists, anarchists, and other groups regularly accused the police of spying on meetings, infiltrating clubs, and stifling free speech—echoing earlier absolute-monarchy practices.
- **Ethnic Minorities**: Irish immigrants in England or other diasporas in major cities reported discriminatory treatment, particularly after incidents like Fenian bombings or other politically charged crimes.

These mixed views underscored that while policing had gained broader legitimacy in Victorian society, conflict and critiques of bias remained a fundamental challenge.

5.3. The "Peelian Principles" Evolving

Robert Peel's original concepts—that police are the public and vice versa—still guided official rhetoric. Many Victorian chiefs constable or commissioners repeated these principles, striving for consensus-based policing. However, real-world conditions—poverty, strikes, moral crackdowns—tested how genuinely they could be practiced. Nonetheless, the core idea that police legitimacy depended on public support persisted as a guiding ideal.

6. International Resonance of Victorian Reforms

6.1. Continental Europe

Countries across Europe observed British policing successes:

- **France**: While it maintained a more centralized tradition (including the gendarmerie), city police in Paris, Lyon, and Marseille adopted structured beats and detective branches. Victorian moral policing found parallels in the "mœurs" police units that monitored prostitution and vice.
- **Germany**: Urban forces in Berlin, Hamburg, and elsewhere balanced militaristic discipline (a holdover from Prussian traditions) with new detective capabilities akin to Scotland Yard.
- **Scandinavian States**: Smaller kingdoms like Sweden or Denmark gradually professionalized local watch forces, often referencing British training manuals and uniform standards.

6.2. The United States

American cities in the late 19th century, dealing with their own Industrial Age, mirrored Victorian Britain's reforms:

- **Structured Beats and Uniforms**: By the 1870s–1880s, most major U.S. police departments used uniforms, official ranks, and recognized detective units.
- **Moral Policing**: Movements like Prohibition (previews in local "dry" ordinances) and vice raids echoed British moral campaigns.
- **Differences**: The U.S. context, however, remained more decentralized, with wide local variations in policy, training, and corruption. Ethnic tensions, frontier legacies, and the aftermath of the Civil War further distinguished American approaches.

6.3. Other Regions

Even in colonized or semi-colonized areas, Victorian-inspired policing took root:

- **Colonial Administrations**: British officials in India, parts of Africa, and Asia introduced training regimens and hierarchical structures, often mixing them with local paramilitary practices.
- **Japan's Meiji Era**: Japanese envoys studied British and French policing. The resulting police system combined a centralized government approach with local precincts.
- **Latin America**: Countries like Argentina or Brazil, influenced by European advisors, introduced professional forces in major cities—Buenos Aires, Rio de Janeiro—aiming to handle industrial growth, though local political circumstances shaped outcomes.

Thus, the Victorian policing model achieved a global presence, albeit adapted to diverse cultural and political climates.

7. Preparing for the 20th Century: Lingering Issues and Achievements

7.1. Achievements of Victorian Policing

By the dawn of the 20th century, Victorian reforms had yielded:

1. **Professional Structures**: Hierarchical command, specialized detective units, official training, and standardized uniforms.
2. **Stronger Public Services**: Many forces cooperated with municipal agencies (fire, health, sanitation), reflecting an integrated approach to urban governance.
3. **Growth of Accountability Norms**: Though still imperfect, the idea that police should maintain clear records and be subject to civilian oversight was more accepted than in earlier periods.

7.2. Ongoing Challenges

Nevertheless, major challenges persisted:

- **Corruption**: Patronage, bribery, and favoritism had not disappeared; political interference remained a reality.
- **Overreach**: Balancing moral regulation against personal freedoms posed a dilemma, with critics pointing to paternalistic or class-based policing.
- **Limited Diversity**: Police forces were overwhelmingly male, often from similar backgrounds. Ethnic or racial minorities rarely served, which contributed to mistrust in certain neighborhoods.
- **Forensic Gaps**: Methods of evidence collection were still rudimentary, hampering certain investigations. Fingerprinting would only be systematically introduced in British policing in the very late 19th or early 20th century.

7.3. Transition into a New Era

As the Victorian epoch ended in 1901, policing in Britain and similarly evolving countries stood at a crossroads. Society was on the cusp of rapid technological advances (automobiles, better forensic science) and dramatic political shifts (mass democracy, world wars). The relatively stable Victorian model of policing, though widely influential, would face fresh pressures in the 20th century.

Chapter 17

Expansion of Policing in the Late 19th Century

By the final decades of the 19th century, policing had secured a more established role in many societies. The Victorian-era reforms explored in Chapter 16 had a global ripple effect: professional police forces were recognized not only in Europe and North America but also in expanding colonial states and nascent nation-states worldwide. Technological progress—improved rail networks, the spread of the telegraph, and the beginnings of telephone systems—supported the sharing of information, making police work more efficient and interconnected. At the same time, rising nationalism, intensified colonial rule, and inter-imperial rivalries shaped how police were used for security and political control.

In this chapter, we will examine:

1. **Global contexts** shaping late 19th-century policing, including nationalism, colonial governance, and commercial expansion.
2. **Further professionalization** of police institutions, focusing on training schools, rank structures, and specialized units.
3. **Legislative milestones** in various countries that codified policing powers, clarified jurisdiction, and aimed to address corruption or overreach.
4. **Evolving relationships** between police and the urban working classes, marked by strikes, demonstrations, and political agitation.
5. **Developments in investigative techniques**, including the formal adoption of new forensic methods such as fingerprinting and improved criminal identification systems.
6. **Continuing challenges** in accountability and civil liberties, as states weighed public order against the growing demand for political and personal freedoms.

By the close of the 19th century, many observers viewed a strong police establishment as a hallmark of modern governance—yet tensions remained, as the quest for efficient control of crime and disorder often collided with evolving social and political ideals.

1. The Larger Global Context of Late 19th-Century Policing

1.1. Nationalism and Unification Movements

In Europe, the late 1800s witnessed the rise or consolidation of national states:

- **Italy** (unified in 1861) and **Germany** (unified in 1871) had to merge diverse regional polities. Policing in these new nations required bridging cultural and administrative differences. Central governments formed or strengthened national gendarmeries or police corps to promote internal unity.
- **Austria-Hungary** struggled with multi-ethnic tensions. Policing, while nominally under imperial authority, was complicated by local ethnic communities who distrusted Habsburg officials.
- **Balkan States**: Nationalist rebellions against the Ottoman Empire led to independent or semi-independent states (Serbia, Romania, Bulgaria), each forging new police structures. These forces often had paramilitary traits, used both for basic law enforcement and for maintaining shaky political control.

1.2. Colonial Governance

Simultaneously, European empires expanded their territories in Africa, Asia, and the Pacific. Policing in colonial contexts often served dual functions: combatting local resistance and safeguarding economic exploitation:

- **British Empire**: In India, the **Indian Police Act of 1861** reorganized policing after the 1857 rebellion, creating provincial inspectorates and local constables under British superintendents. Similar paramilitary-style forces emerged in parts of Africa, with "native police" commanded by white officers.
- **French Colonial Rule**: The French employed a mixture of regular troops, gendarmes, and local auxiliaries to enforce order in North Africa (Algeria, Tunisia), Indochina, and West Africa. District commissioners or commandants held extensive powers to suppress revolts, collect taxes, and run rudimentary courts.
- **Belgian, German, and Portuguese Colonies**: Other imperial powers followed suit, blending imported European policing frameworks with forced labor systems or corvée projects that demanded a heavy-handed security apparatus.

These colonial police forces were often more militarized than metropolitan forces, tasked with subduing populations and protecting colonial economic interests rather than serving broad public safety in the modern sense.

1.3. Economic Growth and Commercial Security

Late 19th-century capitalism spurred massive international trade. Ports like Hamburg, Marseilles, Bombay (Mumbai), Hong Kong, and Buenos Aires grew into bustling centers of commerce:

- **Protection of Trade**: Dockside theft, smuggling, and sabotage became central concerns. Specialized harbor or river police units patrolled waterways and piers.
- **Rail Security**: In many countries, railway companies hired their own police or watchmen to guard stations and track lines. Collaboration with state or local forces grew more common, especially given the fear of banditry and sabotage.
- **Insurance and Private Agencies**: Insurers sometimes funded or supported police functions that mitigated risk. This era also saw the

expansion of private detective agencies (like Pinkerton in the United States) operating transnationally, investigating fraud or transporting valuables.

Thus, commerce and policing became increasingly intertwined, with private and public interests converging on the need for stable environments conducive to industrial and financial activities.

2. Professionalization of Police Institutions

2.1. Training Academies and Standardized Curricula

By the final quarter of the 19th century, many urban police forces formalized their training procedures:

- **Police Academies**: Major cities (London, Paris, Berlin, Vienna, New York, etc.) established academies or centralized schools where recruits underwent weeks or months of instruction in law, self-defense, and record-keeping.
- **Written Exams**: Some forces introduced basic literacy tests or written exams to gauge recruits' ability to file reports and follow legal procedures.
- **Practical Drills**: Drills in crowd control, firearms (in certain contexts), or the use of less-lethal equipment (batons, whips) became routine. This trend mirrored the quasi-military discipline increasingly common in advanced police institutions.

2.2. Hierarchical Rank Structures

A more explicit rank hierarchy emerged, clarifying lines of command:

- **Chief Constable or Commissioner**: Oversaw the entire force in a city or region, accountable to municipal councils or interior ministries.
- **Superintendents and Inspectors**: Managed divisions or districts, supervising day-to-day operations and specialized units (detectives, traffic, vice squads).
- **Sergeants**: Acted as frontline supervisors, ensuring discipline among rank-and-file officers (constables or patrolmen).

This organizational clarity helped handle large-scale challenges, from civil disturbances to complex criminal rings. However, critics noted that rank hierarchies sometimes led to bureaucracy or inflexibility, particularly when quick local decisions were needed.

2.3. Specialized Units and Branches

As cities grew, specialized subdivisions became more common:

- **Vice and Morals Bureaus**: Focused on prostitution, gambling, and liquor infractions—often responding to Victorian moral codes.
- **Juvenile Departments**: Acknowledging rising concerns about youth crime, some forces designated officers or wards specifically to handle juveniles, though robust juvenile justice systems were still on the horizon.
- **Mounted Police**: Retaining cavalry traditions, mounted officers in big European or American cities patrolled large parks, responded to riots, or handled ceremonial duties.
- **Railway or Transit Police**: With rail networks expanding, entire departments specialized in preventing theft of cargo, sabotage of rail lines, or public disorder in stations.

These branching structures revealed how policing was no longer a single, uniform function—forces diversified to address the multifaceted demands of late 19th-century urban life.

3. Legislative Milestones and Policing Authority

3.1. Legal Foundations

Multiple countries passed new statutes defining police authority more precisely:

- **Britain**: Acts like the **Police Act of 1890** fine-tuned retirement benefits, rank definitions, and the scope of local police powers. This official recognition fortified policing as a permanent, professional institution.
- **France**: Successive governments—Monarchy, Republic, or Empire—issued decrees that strengthened the roles of the **préfet de police** in Paris and prefects in the provinces, clarifying their powers over detective work, public gatherings, and moral policing.
- **German Empire**: After unification in 1871, the imperial government let constituent states (like Prussia, Bavaria, Saxony) keep their own police traditions. However, national security laws, especially under Otto von

Bismarck, targeted socialism and certain political movements. Police thus gained enhanced surveillance powers over radical groups.

3.2. Addressing Corruption and Misuse

Exposés of police corruption or brutality spurred further legislation:

- **Transparency Measures**: Some parliaments required annual police reports, showing budgets, arrest statistics, and disciplinary records. Press coverage of these reports could sway public opinion and lead to calls for reform.
- **Limitations on Force**: Certain laws tried to restrict lethal force to grave situations, though enforcement varied. Police training manuals emphasized minimal necessary force, but local practices could deviate.
- **Appeals and Courts**: Governments refined systems by which citizens could contest wrongful arrest or police misconduct in ordinary courts, placing nominal checks on police authority.

Although these legal changes did not eliminate abuse, they signaled a broader intent to regulate the powers of an increasingly potent institution.

3.3. The Growth of Unions and Police Associations

Though official police unions were not always recognized, informal associations or fraternal orders sometimes pressed for better pay, fair promotions, and more humane working hours. In countries where labor organizing was more accepted, rank-and-file officers occasionally found common cause with other public servants—yet force leadership often feared unionization might politicize the police.

4. Police Relations with Working Classes and Political Movements

4.1. Labor Strikes and Demonstrations

As industrialization intensified, so did worker unrest:

- **Mass Protests**: Late 19th-century Europe and North America witnessed large-scale strikes in industries like textiles, coal mining, steel, and

railroads. Police were regularly called to manage picket lines or quell violence if scuffles broke out.
- **Public Order Policing**: Forces developed crowd-control tactics, sometimes forming "reserve squads" or equipping officers with truncheons to disperse rioters.
- **Backlash**: Violent police interventions—such as the Haymarket affair (Chicago, 1886) or the suppression of strikes in France's mining regions—led to accusations that police served capital over community, fueling left-wing distrust.

4.2. Socialist and Anarchist Agitation

Political radicals, including anarchists, socialists, and early communists, used public meetings, pamphlets, and street marches to critique capitalist society:

- **Police Surveillance**: Authorities assigned detectives to infiltrate radical clubs, track printing presses, and monitor foreign agitators crossing borders. Some governments introduced anti-sedition laws, empowering police to shut down "subversive" gatherings.
- **Cross-Border Collaboration**: European powers, wary of anarchist bombings or assassination attempts, occasionally shared intelligence. High-profile incidents (e.g., the assassination of Italy's King Umberto I in 1900 by an anarchist) heightened fear of terrorist plots, spurring more intrusive policing.
- **Response from Radicals**: In turn, radicals denounced police "spies" and insisted that law enforcement stifled legitimate dissent. Clashes erupted in industrial suburbs and working-class neighborhoods, sometimes resulting in arrests en masse.

4.3. Emergence of a "Public Dialogue"

Newspapers, pamphlets, and political cartoons shaped how the working classes, middle classes, and elites viewed the police. While some editorials praised law enforcement's role in maintaining order, others lambasted real or perceived brutality. This ferment underscored how policing had become deeply enmeshed in broader social and political struggles—far from a purely neutral arbiter of law.

5. Advancements in Investigative Techniques and Forensics

5.1. Formal Adoption of Fingerprinting

One of the hallmark innovations of the late 19th century was fingerprint identification:

- **Origins**: Although ancient cultures recognized unique handprints, the method gained modern traction in British-administered India (1850s onward) for verifying contracts. By the 1880s and 1890s, scholars in Europe explored fingerprint patterns scientifically.
- **Breakthrough Figures**: Francis Galton in Britain published major works (e.g., *Finger Prints* in 1892), standardizing classification systems. Argentina became an early adopter in law enforcement.
- **Spread to Other Forces**: By the very end of the 19th century, a handful of police departments in Britain, France, and North America began experimenting with fingerprint records. Although not yet universally accepted, it signaled the future of personal identification beyond "Bertillonage" (anthropometry).

5.2. Refinement of Bertillonage

Before fingerprinting took hold, Alphonse Bertillon's anthropometric system dominated detective bureaus:

- **Measurements**: Officers measured suspects' heights, arm spans, head size, ear shape, etc. The compiled data aimed to identify repeat offenders reliably.
- **Mug Shots**: Bertillon also popularized the front and profile photograph for police files, greatly enhancing suspect identification.
- **Limitations**: Anthropometry sometimes produced errors if measurements were off or if physical features changed with age or health issues. Nevertheless, it was a milestone in systematic record-keeping until fingerprints ultimately supplanted it.

5.3. Systematic Criminal Registers and Communication

The telegraph and, in some urban centers, nascent telephone lines facilitated faster sharing of suspect descriptions and stolen property alerts:

- **Wanted Posters**: Printing technologies improved, allowing police to circulate photographic or illustrated bulletins.
- **International Cooperation**: While formal global agencies like Interpol would not arrive until the early 20th century, some cross-border crime conferences or bilateral treaties emerged, letting detectives share essential data (especially about anarchists or major fugitives).
- **Criminalistics**: Late 19th-century interest in toxins, bullet trajectory, and other evidence laid a foundation for modern forensic science, though full-fledged labs were still rare.

These investigative milestones signaled the transition from merely reactive policing to methodical detection, forging the image of the detective as a specialized expert.

6. Accountability and Civil Liberties in Transition

6.1. Critiques of Political Policing

As states grew stronger, so did their capacity for surveillance. Many intellectuals, newspapers, and opposition politicians complained about:

- **Espionage Against Dissidents**: Under the guise of security, police spied on labor unions, journalists, and reform groups. Countries like Russia's Tsarist regime maintained notorious secret police (the Okhrana) targeting revolutionaries.
- **Harsh Repression**: Police or gendarmes might break up peaceful gatherings or arrest activists without trial. Clashes during suffrage rallies (especially in Britain from the 1890s onward) highlighted potential abuses of power.
- **Legal Reforms**: Some parliaments debated bills limiting preemptive arrests or requiring police warrants for raids. These debates revealed a mounting tension between a desire for order and public demands for freedom of speech and assembly.

6.2. Growth of Civilian Oversight Movements

Inspired by liberal or democratic ideals, certain cities established or strengthened oversight committees:

- **Local Watch Committees**: In Britain, for instance, borough councils oversaw police budgets, appointments, and discipline, ensuring some measure of civilian input.
- **Press Investigations**: High-profile newspapers ran investigative series on alleged misconduct, spurring official inquiries.
- **Social Organizations**: Middle-class philanthropic societies sometimes lobbied for "police reform from within," championing training, moral instruction for officers, and guidelines that prioritized nonviolent interventions.

Though these oversight efforts were modest, they marked the late 19th century as a pivotal time when societies began grappling more consciously with the balance between robust policing and constitutional protections.

6.3. The Seeds of Human Rights Discourse

Although the formal language of "human rights" was still embryonic, a few legal philosophers and politicians started to articulate principles restricting government intrusion. The late 19th century saw early references to the "rights of man" in contexts such as:

- **Freedom from Arbitrary Arrest**: Echoing older Enlightenment traditions, some activists demanded the codification of due process in everyday policing.
- **Protection of Privacy**: Tools like house-to-house searches, mail interception, or forced testimony triggered resistance, especially in more liberal states.
- **Anti-Torture Sentiment**: While judicial torture had been largely abolished in Europe, some colonized regions faced brutal police methods, prompting sporadic criticism from humanitarian observers.

Though far from universal or comprehensive, these rumblings laid groundwork for 20th-century civil liberties campaigns.

7. Late 19th-Century Policing in the United States

7.1. Big City Departments

In major American cities—New York, Chicago, Philadelphia, Boston—policing responded to waves of immigration, industrial strife, and political corruption:

- **Political Patronage**: Ties to local party "machines" remained strong; many officers owed their positions to ward bosses. This led to selective enforcement, especially around election times or for businesses allied with influential politicians.
- **Riots and Strikes**: The Great Railroad Strike (1877), the Haymarket affair (1886), and the Pullman Strike (1894) showcased pitched battles between police (often aided by state militias or Pinkerton agents) and aggrieved workers.
- **Incremental Reforms**: By the 1890s, progressive-minded mayors or commissioners in some cities launched anti-graft campaigns, introduced entrance exams, and created detective bureaus along lines similar to Europe.

7.2. Policing the American South

Post–Civil War "Reconstruction" (1865–1877) had brought federal troops and Freedmen's Bureau agents to uphold rights for formerly enslaved people. But as federal support waned:

- **Local Sheriffs and Police**: Many southern jurisdictions reverted to enforcing Jim Crow laws, suppressing Black political participation through intimidation and selective arrest.
- **Racially Biased Enforcement**: Vagrancy laws targeted Black citizens, enabling forced labor in convict-lease systems. This dynamic was a stark departure from more conventional policing in other regions, revealing how policing structures could be harnessed for racial subjugation.

7.3. Western Territories and Frontier Policing

As the frontier era dwindled, territorial or newly minted state governments established:

- **Ranger Forces**: States like Texas continued deploying "Rangers" with broad policing mandates, blending paramilitary and investigative roles.
- **Mining and Cattle Town Police**: Vigilante groups or private security gave way, in some cases, to town marshals or small city police departments.
- **Federal Marshals**: For interstate crimes—train robberies, mail theft—U.S. Marshals or Treasury/Secret Service agents took on expanded roles. They pursued famous outlaws like the Dalton Gang or Butch Cassidy's crew, shaping the mythos of the "Wild West."

By century's end, industrialization had penetrated many Western states, prompting further professionalization of local forces, though vestiges of frontier-style justice persisted in remote areas.

8. Preparing for the New Century: Key Takeaways

8.1. Consolidated Policing as a "Civilized Norm"

Throughout Europe, North America, and increasingly in colonial regions, the notion of stable, professional policing took hold as a marker of state maturity. Government reports lauded the achievements of new detective units, scientific identification methods, and the improved discipline of uniformed officers.

8.2. Persistent Conflicts

Late 19th-century societies still wrestled with fundamental questions:

- **Fairness and Accountability**: Citizens demanded checks on police power. Corruption and brutality remained thorny issues.

- **Class and Racial Bias**: Policing often enforced social hierarchies, stoking discontent among marginalized communities.
- **Political Uses of the Police**: States employed policing for both legitimate crime control and the suppression of dissent, creating a dual identity for law enforcement—as both protective and repressive, depending on perspective.

8.3. Impetus for Future Changes

Looking beyond 1900, the seeds were planted for transformations in the early 20th century:

- **Unionization and Professional Associations**: Police themselves began to form societies or associations demanding better pay, consistent training, and recognition.
- **Advanced Forensics**: Fingerprinting's formal acceptance, plus emergent ballistics and other methods, promised more precise crime solving.
- **Broadening Oversight**: Civil society groups, philanthropic bodies, and newspapers increasingly scrutinized police actions. In some places, governments pondered creating ombudsman-like offices or more formal civilian review boards—though significant adoption would come much later.

In sum, policing on the eve of the 20th century had reached a watershed: recognized as essential but still contending with socio-political tensions, uneven standards, and debates about its fundamental purpose in a rapidly changing world.

Chapter 18

Shifts in Policing Approaches Near the Turn of the 20th Century

As the 19th century drew to a close, many of the social, economic, and political forces that had shaped policing—industrialization, nationalism, colonial expansion—continued to intensify. Simultaneously, new currents of thought and technology were on the horizon. Progressive political movements sought to curtail corruption and champion social welfare, while socialist and labor organizations pressured governments to address systemic inequalities. Technological advances, such as the telephone and improved transportation, further accelerated communication and mobility, impacting how police responded to crime.

In this chapter, we will explore:

1. **Influential political and social movements**—progressivism, socialism, women's suffrage—that pressed for changes in policing roles and oversight.
2. **The evolving concept of "public service"** in police work, as modern states weighed moral duties against the need for control over restive populations.
3. **Continuing developments in investigative techniques**, including the initial introduction of fingerprinting and expansions of detective bureaus.
4. **Debates over policing tactics**—crowd control, intelligence gathering, militarized response—and the line between legitimate security and political oppression.
5. **Early examples of transnational cooperation** or cross-border pursuits, anticipating more formal international policing frameworks in the 20th century.
6. **Lasting dilemmas** of accountability, bias, and the tension between local autonomy and centralized authority that remained unresolved as the new century began.

While major transformations of the 20th century—two world wars, mass democracy, advanced forensic science—lie beyond our current scope, the seeds of these developments were already visible in policing structures and philosophies around 1900. Examining these transitional years reveals how policing was on the cusp of becoming the institution recognizable in more contemporary times.

1. Progressive Political Movements and Policing

1.1. The Progressive Era in the United States

In the U.S., the **Progressive Era** (roughly 1890s–1920) sought to reform politics, curb corruption, and improve social conditions:

- **Municipal Reforms**: Progressive mayors or governors implemented civil service exams for police recruitment, limiting the grip of party machines. Some introduced police commissions with civilian members, aiming for impartial oversight.
- **Settlement Houses and Community Efforts**: Figures like Jane Addams (Hull House in Chicago) championed cooperation between social workers and police, believing that addressing poverty would reduce crime. Police were encouraged to handle minor issues with a more humanitarian approach rather than pure enforcement.
- **Temperance and Morality**: Progressives often supported anti-alcohol campaigns, pushing police to raid saloons or illegal "speakeasies" (though full Prohibition at the federal level would come in 1920). This moral dimension echoed Victorian values but in a distinctly American context.

1.2. European Social Reformers

In Europe, parallel currents emerged:

- **Urban Welfare Measures**: Certain municipalities established slum clearance programs, public baths, or cheap lodging for migrant workers, believing social improvements would lighten the police burden.
- **Anti-Corruption Drives**: Progressives in city councils across Britain, France, and Germany demanded transparent accounting of police funds, fair disciplinary procedures, and clearer definitions of officer powers.
- **Women's Activism**: In Britain, women activists calling for suffrage or labor rights encountered police crackdowns at demonstrations. Over time, their lobbying spurred discussions about female officers or special units to handle cases involving women and children—a nascent idea around 1900.

1.3. Socialism and Labor Movements

Socialist and labor parties, expanding their influence in legislative bodies, pressured governments to decriminalize certain labor actions, end brutal strike-breaking, and permit peaceful assembly:

- **Legal Reforms**: Some countries passed laws that allowed "authorised" demonstrations or restricted police from using lethal force except in dire circumstances.
- **Polarized Atmospheres**: Conservative factions insisted on harsh measures against what they deemed "subversive" socialism, causing friction within police leadership as top officers balanced political directives with emerging liberal norms.
- **Unionization of Police** (Limited): Embryonic forms of police unionism or associations cropped up, but many governments resisted. If police unionized, states feared they could side with strikers or hamper public order. Nonetheless, the debate indicated a shift toward viewing police as workers with rights, not mere instruments of the state.

2. Evolving Concept of Public Service in Policing

2.1. Policing as Civic Duty

Late 19th-century discourses emphasized that the police, rather than being a purely repressive force, had responsibilities to serve:

- **Aid and Assistance**: Officers increasingly engaged in non-criminal tasks, from providing first aid at accidents to guiding lost children or giving directions to newcomers. This "friendly bobby" model was held up particularly in Britain as an ideal of community policing.
- **Health and Hygiene**: In major cities, some forces took on quasi-sanitary roles, reporting epidemics or ensuring that quarantines were obeyed.
- **Moral "Policing"**: While controversial, many city forces responded to demands for decency—monitoring public bathing areas, musical performances, or dance halls. Their presence supposedly ensured events remained "respectable."

2.2. The Tension Between Service and Control

However, tensions arose where paternalistic or moralizing tasks overlapped with broader state power:

- **Class-Based Enforcement**: Middle-class "improvement" campaigns sometimes resulted in heavy policing of working-class leisure venues or informal economies (e.g., street vendors, hawkers).
- **Political Strikes**: Police faced the dilemma of whether their role was to protect all citizens equally or to defend property and business interests when strikes turned heated.
- **Overlapping Roles**: The line between caretaker and enforcer was blurry. Some critics accused police of being too lenient with moral "offenses" while ignoring deeper socio-economic ills—others complained they harassed petty offenders for minor infractions.

Yet the emerging rhetoric that police should "serve and protect" the public at large hinted at a shift in legitimacy, setting the stage for more community-oriented policing philosophies in the 20th century.

3. Continuing Developments in Investigative Techniques

3.1. Fingerprinting Goes Mainstream

By the early 1900s, fingerprinting was no longer just an experimental method:

- **Argentina and the Rojas Case (1892)**: A landmark case in Argentina used fingerprints to convict a suspect for murder, drawing international attention.
- **Britain**: Scotland Yard officially adopted fingerprint classification around 1901, thanks to pioneers like Edward Henry, who refined Galton's system.
- **Diffusion to Other Forces**: Major European cities and some American departments began establishing fingerprint bureaus, though it would take years for smaller towns or colonial outposts to catch up.

3.2. Enhanced Criminal Registries

Detective bureaus continued refining record-keeping:

- **Criminal Anthropometry vs. Fingerprints**: Many departments maintained both systems for a time, cross-referencing Bertillon measurements with fingerprint sets.
- **Central Bureaus**: Nations like France and Germany developed centralized archives in their capitals, enabling police from different regions to request suspect files or identify traveling criminals.
- **Photography and Mug Shots**: Photography had become routine in large stations, generating troves of images for cross-comparison. Though limited by inconsistent lighting or angles, the concept of a visual "rogues' gallery" was now widely accepted.

3.3. Media Sensationalism and Detective Mystique

Late 19th-century newspapers avidly reported on sensational crimes—murders, bank heists, or daring burglaries—feeding the public fascination with detective work:

- **True Crime Stories**: Publishers realized that stories about cunning detectives and dramatic arrests sold well. Writers and editors sometimes lionized or vilified police, influencing public perception.
- **Fiction and Inspiration**: Literary figures such as Arthur Conan Doyle's Sherlock Holmes (introduced in 1887) stirred immense interest in deductive methods, magnifying the detective's heroic aura.
- **Pressure on Police**: With the public enthralled by detective tales, real officers faced mounting expectations to solve high-profile crimes swiftly and with cunning skill, occasionally leading to hasty or misguided investigations under media glare.

This synergy between investigative progress and cultural representation further entrenched the detective's role as a specialized, almost romantic figure in law enforcement.

4. Debates Over Tactics: Crowd Control and Surveillance

4.1. Crowd Control Innovations

With large labor rallies, suffrage demonstrations, or nationalist marches becoming frequent, forces refined crowd-control strategies:

- **Riot Drills**: Some city forces arranged specialized platoons who trained in "shield and baton" formations, designed to push back or split large gatherings.
- **Mounted Units**: Still vital, mounted police could quickly break up crowds. This method drew criticism if used aggressively, especially against peaceful protesters.
- **Use of Firearms**: Police in many European states seldom carried guns on routine patrols, but riot squads sometimes had access to rifles, used only under official orders. In the U.S., firearms were more common, raising the risk of lethal escalation during civil unrest.

4.2. Political Surveillance

As socialist, anarchist, and nationalist movements spread, states demanded broader intelligence gathering:

- **Infiltration**: Undercover officers joined radical meetings to identify ringleaders or gather evidence. While effective, it fueled accusations of entrapment and manipulative policing.
- **Secret Files**: Some governments (e.g., Tsarist Russia, Wilhelmine Germany) compiled extensive dossiers on suspected agitators, stored at central security bureaus.
- **Coordination Across Borders**: Anarchist violence—bombings, assassinations—pushed European police to exchange data on known extremists. While not a formal alliance, this embryonic cooperation prefigured later international policing bodies.

4.3. Public Concern

Politically minded citizens, especially liberals and social democrats, decried state overreach:

- **Civil Liberties**: Writers and campaigners complained about random searches, infiltration of peaceful groups, and potential for framing activists.
- **Legal Frameworks**: Some parliaments in Western Europe introduced mild restrictions, requiring judicial warrants for certain investigative actions—though enforcement was uneven.
- **Polarization**: Conservatives praised robust policing as essential for stability. Radicals claimed it was oppression. This schism over how far policing could go to preempt dissident threats foreshadowed 20th-century debates about domestic security vs. personal freedoms.

5. Early Steps Toward Transnational Cooperation

5.1. Cross-Border Pursuits

Criminals increasingly took advantage of relaxed passport regimes in parts of Europe or hopped steamships to foreign ports:

- **Hot Pursuit Policies**: Some bilateral agreements allowed pursuit of suspects a short distance over borders, provided local authorities were alerted.
- **Extradition Treaties**: More nations negotiated treaties outlining the return of fugitives for certain crimes, though political offenses were often excluded.
- **Ad Hoc Arrangements**: Detectives sometimes traveled covertly to track criminals, relying on personal contacts in foreign police forces. This practice was informal and risked diplomatic uproars if discovered.

5.2. Conferences and Exchanges

Even without a formal international police agency, occasional conferences or correspondence networks formed:

- **Anarchist Threat**: In the 1890s, European states, alarmed by anarchist assassinations, convened ad hoc meetings to discuss intelligence sharing.
- **Expositions and Exhibitions**: World's fairs or specialized congresses (e.g., the 1900 Exposition in Paris) served as opportunities for police officials to exchange ideas on training, detective methods, and management.
- **Early Communication Tools**: Telegraph cables across continents made it feasible to wire urgent bulletins about wanted suspects. The telephone, while still restricted to urban elites, slowly entered police stations, enabling faster local responses.

Though modest, these cross-border steps sowed the seeds of more structured international policing collaboration that would emerge in the 20th century under bodies like Interpol.

6. Lingering Dilemmas as 1900 Approached

6.1. Accountability Mechanisms

Despite some oversight committees and legal constraints, accountability was patchy:

- **Executive Influence**: In many countries, interior ministries exerted heavy control over police policy, overshadowing local input.
- **Public Commissions**: Investigations into brutality or corruption were often one-off responses to scandal, rather than permanent checks.

- **Court Systems**: Courts sometimes voided questionable police actions (unlawful searches, false arrests), but litigation was cumbersome for average citizens, limiting its deterrent effect on misconduct.

6.2. Class and Racial Bias Unresolved

While philanthropic and progressive voices demanded more equitable policing:

- **Ethnic Minorities**: In diverse empires—Austro-Hungarian, Russian, Ottoman—minority groups often faced disproportionate scrutiny. Pogroms against Jewish communities in Russia sometimes happened with police complicity or passivity.
- **Colonial Populations**: The gap between colonizers and colonized was stark. Colonial forces upheld laws that favored settler economic interests, with minimal concern for local welfare.
- **Urban Poor**: Welfare organizations might press for leniency, yet police crackdowns on vagrants, petty thieves, or homeless populations remained routine.

6.3. Technological Potential vs. Constraints

Though the telephone, fingerprinting, and even early automobiles were on the horizon, real adoption was slow:

- **Infrastructure Limits**: Rural districts lacked telephones or electric lighting, hampering quick response times.
- **Cost and Training**: Many departments lacked funds or know-how for advanced forensic labs or widespread telephone lines.
- **Social Reluctance**: Some localities resisted new technology out of distrust or fear of privacy invasion (telephones enabling mass surveillance, etc.).

Hence, while the late 19th century was an era of innovation, the full potential for technologically driven policing would require the 20th century's expanded infrastructure.

7. Envisioning the Twentieth Century

7.1. Seeds of Modernization

As 1900 neared, observers predicted further transformations:

- **Centralization**: More integrated national police systems, especially in newly unified states, would streamline training, record-sharing, and investigative techniques.
- **Science and Policing**: The idea that policing could be more scientific—through systematized forensics, criminology research, and psychological studies of crime—took root in academic circles.
- **Community Engagement**: Some reformers envisioned a policing style that balanced enforcement with social service, anticipating proto-community policing ideas.

7.2. Impending Shocks

Unbeknownst to those living at the time, the early 20th century would bring:

- **World Wars**: Massive militarization, demands for domestic security, and surveillance expansions beyond anything the late 19th century had seen.
- **Revolutions and Political Upheavals**: Russia's 1917 revolution, upheaval across Central Europe post–World War I, and decolonization movements worldwide would drastically shift policing mandates and alignments.
- **Global Communication**: Radio technology, improvements in roads, and the eventual rise of automobiles would revolutionize rapid response and inter-city cooperation.

But these events lay ahead. In 1900, policing stood at a crossroads, shaped by the era's modernization yet constrained by older social orders and incomplete accountability frameworks.

Chapter 19

Policing and Societal Change (Late 19th to Early 20th Centuries)

We have traced how policing evolved from ancient watches and feudal constables to more structured, professional forces across the globe by the late 19th century. Chapter 18 illustrated a turning point: the cusp of the 20th century, when new technologies, political ideologies, and social pressures were already reshaping the institution of law enforcement. Before we conclude this survey, we must look more closely at how these transitions in the late 19th to early 20th centuries—roughly from the 1880s through the opening decades of the 1900s—continued to influence policing philosophies, practices, and structures.

In this chapter, we will explore:

1. **Wider political and cultural shifts**—including mass politics, early women's suffrage efforts, and evolving media—that sparked new debates about the scope and tactics of policing.
2. **The deepening role of scientific thought**, where criminology, early psychology, and further forensic developments began to alter assumptions about crime prevention and investigation.
3. **Nation-building efforts** in newly unified or reorganized states, where police were central to forging national identity and stability.
4. **Colonial policing** at its height, as European powers solidified control overseas, using paramilitary police to manage labor, quell revolts, and impose new economic systems.
5. **Gradual steps toward transnational cooperation**, as officials recognized that criminals and political agitators ignored borders, prompting early exchanges of data or suspect records.
6. **Persistent social inequalities**—class, race, gender—and how these shaped public perceptions of policing, especially in fast-changing urban environments.

While the world of the 1910s and beyond would see cataclysmic events such as World War I and worldwide ideological revolutions, the seeds of those upheavals were already present in the policing landscape, revealing how law enforcement stood at a historical crossroads.

1. Mass Politics, Reform, and Suffrage Movements

1.1. Expansion of Voting Rights

In many countries, the late 19th century witnessed a broader inclusion of the working classes and, in some contexts, women (though female suffrage came later in most places):

- **Male Suffrage**: Britain's Reform Acts (especially 1867, 1884) substantially increased the male electorate, giving more citizens political leverage over local and national decisions—including those about policing budgets or appointments.
- **Women's Suffrage Campaigns**: While full suffrage for women in major powers typically came after World War I, the late 19th century saw rising activism. Groups like the Women's Social and Political Union in Britain staged demonstrations and acts of civil disobedience. Police responses could be forceful (arrests, forced feeding of hunger strikers in prison), fueling debate about the proper use of police power against protesters, particularly women.

1.2. New Political Parties

Social democratic and labor parties, growing in Germany, France, Britain, Scandinavia, and beyond, pushed for state accountability and protection of workers' rights. Their increased representation in parliaments meant:

- **Legislative Scrutiny**: Police budgets, officer recruitment policies, and handling of strikes were publicly debated. Some socialist lawmakers demanded more peaceful, mediating approaches to large protests.
- **Civil Liberties Emphasis**: Politicians challenged vague "subversion" laws that had once justified broad police powers. They insisted on clearer judicial oversight to prevent arbitrary arrests.
- **Class Tension**: Meanwhile, conservative factions feared police "softness" might embolden radicals. They defended strong enforcement tactics, stoking polarizing debates in the press and government halls.

These dynamics forced police authorities to navigate conflicting political agendas, sometimes shifting policies depending on which party held power locally or nationally.

2. Influence of Scientific Thought and Early Criminology

2.1. The Emergence of Criminology

Thinkers like Cesare Lombroso (in Italy), Enrico Ferri, and Raffaele Garofalo pioneered "positivist criminology," suggesting that criminal behavior might stem from biological or social factors beyond mere moral failing:

- **"Born Criminal" Ideas**: Lombroso's work argued that certain physical traits or atavistic features predisposed individuals to crime. Though widely criticized later, his theories sparked new discussions about using scientific measurements (head shape, facial angles) to identify potential criminals.
- **Social Environment**: Some criminologists, conversely, highlighted poverty, broken families, or urban squalor as prime drivers of crime—pushing police to engage more with social reforms.
- **Impact on Policing**: While many officers had limited exposure to academic theories, some high-ranking officials integrated these ideas, believing advanced classification and data-collection (like anthropometry) could help predict or deter crime.

2.2. Early Psychological Approaches

Alongside physical theories, a budding interest in psychological traits or pathologies influenced detective methods:

- **Interview Techniques**: Investigators experimented with questioning styles that probed suspects' emotions or mental states, seeking confessions through empathy or cunning rather than brute force.
- **Debates on Responsibility**: Courts and police sometimes confronted mentally ill offenders, prompting questions about whether prisons or asylums were the proper solution. This tension nudged policing to differentiate between "criminal" and "mentally disordered," though resources for psychiatric evaluation were scarce.
- **Child Offenders**: Some jurisdictions began distinguishing juvenile from adult criminals, reflecting a shift toward reform-oriented policing and specialized youth facilities.

Though crude by modern standards, these developments hinted that policing might become not just a matter of physical order but also a domain informed by scientific insights into human behavior.

3. Nation-Building and Centralized Policing

3.1. Latecomers to Unification

States like Italy (fully unified by 1871 with Rome's annexation) and Germany (1871) continued forging cohesive identities through:

- **National Police Systems**: The Italian government strove to standardize the **Carabinieri** (a gendarmerie-like force) and local polizie across regions that had distinct traditions. In Germany, Prussia's influential model guided policing in other states, although local autonomy persisted.
- **Symbolic Representation**: Uniformed officers represented state authority at local ceremonies and public holidays. They projected the image of a strong, unified nation.
- **Challenges of Regionalism**: In southern Italy or certain German principalities, older loyalties and banditry traditions lingered, forcing police to adapt. Some areas welcomed national oversight; others resented what they saw as an imposition of external control.

3.2. Shifting Imperial Boundaries

Elsewhere, multi-ethnic empires like Austro-Hungary or Russia found themselves:

- **Suppressing Minority Aspirations**: Policing in the Russian Empire cracked down on Polish, Baltic, or Ukrainian nationalist movements. Austria-Hungary faced similar unrest among Czechs, Slovaks, South Slavs.
- **Paramilitary Policing**: Gendarmerie or cossack units often combined policing with military duties, swiftly crushing rebellions or demonstrations.
- **Strain on Resources**: Frequent uprisings or sabotage efforts meant large budgets for internal security, overshadowing social or service-oriented roles for the police.

These empire-level challenges underscored how policing could be a unifying state function—or a repressive tool to maintain contested borders and quell ethnic dissent.

4. Colonial Policing at Its Height

4.1. Tightening Control Over Colonies

By the late 19th century, the "Scramble for Africa" and further expansions in Asia and the Pacific solidified European imperial spheres:

- **Paramilitary Style**: In British colonies, forces like the **King's African Rifles** or the Indian district police exhibited a military ethos, focusing on tax collection, labor "recruitment," and quelling uprisings.
- **Association vs. Direct Rule**: The French in West Africa often used local chiefs under a policy of "association" but maintained garrisons of colonial police or tirailleurs (colonial infantry) to ensure compliance.
- **Use of Indigenous Auxiliaries**: Colonial authorities frequently recruited local men for rank-and-file policing, while Europeans held commanding ranks. This structure sometimes exacerbated tribal or ethnic rivalries, as certain groups were favored over others.

4.2. Impact on Indigenous Societies

Colonial policing fundamentally altered local governance:

- **Undermining Traditional Justice**: Systems of mediation by elders or clan heads were sidelined in favor of foreign codes. Indigenous policing customs were labeled "primitive," though colonial officers often borrowed from them for convenience.
- **Forced Labor and Punitive Expeditions**: Protesters or villages that resisted rubber quotas, cash-crop demands, or railway projects faced brutal collective punishments, including floggings and burnings of homes.
- **Debate in Europe**: Occasional humanitarian critics at home decried stories of abuses (e.g., the Congo Free State atrocities), but official accountability was limited. Colonies often operated with wide discretion, overshadowed by imperial economic agendas.

4.3. Seeds of Future Resistance

While colonial policing repressed immediate revolts, it also spurred nationalist consciousness:

- **Intellectual Elites**: Educated locals, sometimes employed in lower-level police or administrative roles, witnessed colonial injustice firsthand, fueling nationalist sentiments.
- **Urban Migrants**: Cities in colonies saw a mix of ethnicities, new jobs, and political discussion clubs—police infiltration of these clubs heightened local distrust of colonial regimes.
- **Post-WWII Momentum** (beyond our scope): These late 19th-century experiences foreshadowed the mid-20th-century independence movements, in which colonial policing legacies became flashpoints for calls to dismantle oppressive structures.

5. Steps Toward International Policing Cooperation

5.1. Early Crime-Fighting Conventions

Although formal international organizations were still nascent, high-profile crimes crossing borders pressed officials to communicate:

- **Anarchist Threat**: European interior ministries, alarmed by bombings and assassinations, quietly exchanged suspect lists. The 1898 Rome Conference tackled international anarchism, leading to proposals for data-sharing.

- **Smuggling Networks**: Customs and police cooperated on anti-smuggling efforts in major ports, sometimes pooling intelligence on contraband routes (drugs, arms, illicit goods).
- **Bilateral Agreements**: Countries like France and Belgium drafted treaties clarifying extradition for serious crimes—murder, forgery, major theft—while disclaiming purely political offenses.

5.2. Foundations of a Global Police Community

By 1900, a nascent sense that "crime knows no borders" was taking hold:

- **Professional Circles**: Senior detectives or commissioners at expositions or criminal congresses began forging personal networks.
- **Common Forensic Methods**: Fingerprinting and anthropometry established technical standards that transcended language barriers.
- **Emerging Models**: Some officials dreamt of an international bureau to share bulletins and photos—an idea that would materialize decades later as Interpol (founded in 1923, beyond our timeframe).

Though rudimentary, these cross-border links indicated that policing was gradually becoming an international concern, not solely a domestic matter.

6. Persistent Dilemmas as the 19th Century Ends

6.1. Corruption, Political Bias, and Brutality

Despite progressive ideals:

- **Embedded Corruption**: Local political machines, racial or class prejudices, and lenient discipline meant corruption was hardly eradicated. Journalists continued uncovering "scandals," but reforms could be stalled by bureaucratic inertia.
- **Political Policing**: Repeated clampdowns on socialists, anarchists, and independence activists demonstrated the continuing use of police as a political tool. Public controversies arose whenever alleged subversives claimed innocence, igniting debates about free expression.
- **Excessive Force**: Riot policing occasionally ended in fatalities—whether in Chicago's labor rallies or in rural European locales resisting new tax laws. Each incident underscored unresolved questions about balancing order with humane treatment.

6.2. Social Inequalities and Bias

Victorian and Gilded Age societal structures endured:

- **Unequal Treatment:** The poor, ethnic minorities, or colonial subjects faced heavier surveillance and punishments for minor offenses. Middle-class neighborhoods often enjoyed friendlier "community patrols," highlighting a policing double standard.
- **Women's Issues:** Although some forces employed a handful of female matrons or clerks, policing remained overwhelmingly male, often ill-prepared to handle crimes against women or children with empathy or specialized approaches.
- **Urban Slums:** Police presence in slums typically oscillated between neglect (allowing petty crimes to fester) and crackdowns (raids on alleged vice dens), rarely addressing root causes like unemployment or substandard housing.

6.3. Technological Constraints

Potential for modernization was often limited by:

- **Infrastructure Gaps:** Many rural areas or smaller colonies lacked telegraphs, decent roads, or station houses.
- **Cost of Forensics:** Establishing advanced labs was pricey. Even fingerprinting required training and materials; some departments chose not to invest heavily, relying on older practices.
- **Resistance to Change:** Traditionalist officers or officials viewed new equipment or methods with suspicion, preferring tried-and-tested strategies.

7. Looking Forward: Policing on the Eve of the 20th Century

7.1. Key Accomplishments

Despite the challenges, the progress from the early 19th to the early 20th century was striking:

1. **Institutional Professionalism**: Most major cities had uniformed, hierarchical police forces, recognized as permanent civic structures.
2. **Detective Specialization**: Investigative branches had grown more sophisticated, employing photography, anthropometry, and—slowly—fingerprinting.
3. **Partly Tamed Corruption**: Scandal-driven reforms and some civil service measures had checked the worst forms of graft, though not eliminated them.

7.2. Unresolved Tensions

Yet fundamental questions remained open:

- **Public vs. Political Interests**: To what extent should the police serve the state's stability vs. the people's liberties?
- **Centralization vs. Local Autonomy**: Nations struggled to decide how much policing should be directed by national ministries instead of local municipalities.
- **Scope of Policing**: Should police act as moral guardians, public welfare agents, or strictly enforcers of criminal law?
- **International Crime**: As cross-border commerce and travel expanded, governments glimpsed the necessity for broader cooperation to tackle smuggling, counterfeiting, or extremist groups.

7.3. Impending 20th-Century Turmoil

Few foresaw how the Great War (World War I) and subsequent revolutions would massively rearrange political landscapes, forging new states and dissolving old empires. Policing would be integral to these upheavals, further refined or repurposed by nationalist, fascist, or socialist regimes. The seeds of modern policing—professional, technologically aided, and capable of both service and oppression—were firmly planted by 1900, poised to either flourish or distort under changing ideologies.

Chapter 20

Conclusion: Reflecting on Early and Pre-Modern Policing

Over the preceding nineteen chapters, we have followed the long and winding road of policing history—spanning ancient civilizations, medieval watch systems, the rise of sheriffs and constables, the influences of Enlightenment ideas, Napoleonic centralization, colonial expansions, industrial-era transformations, and the final steps toward the early 20th century. At every stage, policing has reflected the societies that shaped it, serving as both a mechanism for community safety and a tool for maintaining power structures.

In this concluding chapter, we will:

1. **Recap the major eras** and transitions in policing, highlighting the common threads of consolidation, professionalization, and shifting boundaries between public service and political control.
2. **Emphasize the key themes** that recurred throughout history: class and racial biases, corruption and accountability, moral regulation, and the impact of military or paramilitary structures.
3. **Acknowledge the role of external forces**—social, economic, and technological changes—that continuously reshaped policing, from new legal codes to the advent of trains, telegraphs, and early forensic science.
4. **Assess how early policing** set the foundation for modern law enforcement, noting legacies that persisted even into the 20th century and beyond: hierarchical command, uniformed patrols, detective bureaus, moral policing, and debates over civil rights.
5. **Reflect on the enduring tensions**—order vs. liberty, centralization vs. local autonomy, service vs. suppression—that formed the backbone of historical conflicts over policing.
6. **Look forward briefly** to the early modern and modern developments—like the expansion of motorized patrols, the institutionalization of fingerprinting, the rise of international policing cooperation, and the intensification of political policing in totalitarian regimes—while respecting our focus on pre-20th-century roots.

By tracing how policing evolved step by step, we can better understand the complexity of current law enforcement institutions worldwide. The past offers a panoramic view of the struggles and achievements that inform today's debates about police power, reforms, and social justice.

1. Recap of the Major Historical Phases

1.1. Ancient and Classical Roots

From the earliest city-states in Mesopotamia, Egypt, and later Greece and Rome, communities recognized the need for maintaining order, protecting property, and mediating disputes:

- **Temple Guards and Watchmen**: Combining religious, administrative, and military functions, these figures laid a primitive groundwork for later policing roles.
- **Roman Vigiles**: Both firefighters and night watch, they foreshadowed the concept of dedicated municipal patrols.
- **Military Overlaps**: Early forms of law enforcement often operated under military or noble oversight, reflecting how security was tied to ruling elites.

1.2. Medieval and Feudal Policing

With the collapse of the Western Roman Empire, power fragmented:

- **Local Watch and Ward**: Towns used volunteer or part-time watchmen to keep peace, while rural areas depended on sheriffs, lords, and feudal retainers.
- **Rise of the Sheriff and Constable**: In places like England, these offices bridged the gap between the monarch's authority and local governance, showing how policing was shaped by feudal obligations.
- **Influence of the Church**: Moral and religious enforcement intertwined, with church courts and religious orders contributing to public discipline.

1.3. Early Modern Developments

From the 16th to 18th centuries:

- **Centralizing Monarchies**: Absolute rulers (e.g., in France, Russia) expanded policing to reinforce royal power, employing secret police or militarized units.
- **Colonial Policing Models**: European empires transplanted sheriff/constable systems or paramilitary garrisons into colonies, often aiming to control local populations and secure revenues.

- **Enlightenment Ideas**: Philosophers critiqued abuses, endorsing due process, proportional punishments, and less arbitrary policing—laying intellectual groundwork for reforms.

1.4. Napoleonic and 19th-Century Transformation

The 19th century's industrial growth and Napoleonic administrative models accelerated professional policing:

- **Professional Forces**: Sir Robert Peel's Metropolitan Police Act (1829) in Britain and similar moves on the Continent established permanent, uniformed patrols.
- **Industrial Pressures**: Cities ballooned, intensifying crime fears, labor conflicts, and moral campaigns. Police became mediators in riots, strikes, and daily urban disorder.
- **Detective Work**: Emergence of specialized investigative branches (Scotland Yard, the Sûreté) reflected new techniques like photography, anthropometry, and eventually fingerprinting.
- **Colonial Expansion**: Militarized policing cemented foreign rule, forcing local societies into new forms of subjugation.

1.5. Turn of the 20th Century

By the century's end:

- **Consolidated Institutions**: Policing was widely recognized as a crucial state function.
- **Accountability vs. Authority**: Reforms chipped away at corruption, but political policing and class/racial biases endured.
- **Foundations for Modernity**: Communications (telegraph, phone), standardized training, and rudimentary forensics set the stage for the more technologically advanced policing of the 20th century.

2. Key Themes and Recurring Issues

2.1. Class, Race, and Power

Whether in medieval estates, colonial territories, or industrial capitals, policing often reflected dominant social hierarchies. Elite and ruling classes used law enforcement to protect property and quell unrest. Marginalized groups—peasants, slaves, colonized peoples, ethnic or religious minorities—faced harsher policing, forming a consistent thread of conflict.

2.2. Corruption and Accountability

From petty bribes in medieval towns to "machine politics" in Gilded Age America, corruption infiltrated police ranks. Efforts at reform (inspection boards, civil service exams, journals exposing scandals) recurred, showing a persistent tension between professional ideals and entrenched patronage systems.

2.3. Policing Morality

Societies repeatedly tasked law enforcement with regulating moral behavior—Sabbath laws, public decency, alcohol consumption, prostitution. Critics questioned how far police should intervene in private life, foreshadowing ongoing debates over personal freedoms versus societal norms.

2.4. Public Service vs. Political Tool

The dual identity of policing—protecting communities yet enforcing the ruling powers' agendas—emerged time and again. Secret police or detective branches tracked dissent, while local patrols aided citizens in accidents or investigations. Balancing these roles has never been straightforward.

2.5. Technological and Administrative Evolution

Each era's policing was constrained or enabled by its technology—whether it was the donkey path or the railway, the quill pen or telegraph, or the emergence of fingerprint classification. Administrative reforms (from Napoleonic codifications to Victorian-era training schools) revealed how law enforcement mirrored broader structural shifts in governance.

3. External Forces Shaping Policing

3.1. Social and Economic Shifts

Population booms, urbanization, industrial labor movements—these continuously recast the role of police. Where social injustices festered, policing either attempted mediation or cracked down under elite pressure, fueling deep-rooted perceptions of whose interests the police served.

3.2. Religious and Cultural Frameworks

Whether under Islamic caliphates, Christian monarchies, or Confucian dynasties, policing systems adapted to prevailing religious or ethical codes. The interplay of moral authority with secular power frequently blurred lines, giving police quasi-spiritual or paternalistic duties.

3.3. Wars and Political Upheavals

Major conflicts (such as the Napoleonic Wars or mid-century revolutions) often spurred centralized systems, expanded military-style policing, or triggered reforms afterward. In colonial settings, resistance and revolts shaped harsh paramilitary policing. Every upheaval left legacies in law enforcement structure and ethos.

4. How Early Policing Paved the Way for the Modern Era

4.1. Institutional Foundations

By the late 19th century:

- **Uniformed Patrols**: Recognizable "men in blue" (or other colors) walking beats became a hallmark of urban safety.
- **Command Hierarchies**: Forces refined ranks and bureaus, ensuring some level of internal discipline.
- **Detective Specialties**: The concept of a plainclothes officer trained in investigative methods gained wide acceptance, anticipating modern detective divisions.

4.2. Ancestors of Modern Forensics

Bertillon's measurements, photographic mug shots, and the initial spread of fingerprinting laid groundwork for the explosion of scientific policing in the 20th century—blood typing, DNA analysis, advanced ballistics, digital databases. The late 19th century was thus a transitional phase where science began to supplement hunches and witness testimony.

4.3. International Awareness

Though informal, the seeds of cross-border policing cooperation were planted, anticipating modern frameworks like Interpol. Nations saw that criminals exploited jurisdictional gaps, and political radicals traveled widely, underscoring the future need for standardized communication and extradition protocols.

5. Enduring Tensions in Policing: Lessons from History

5.1. Order vs. Liberty

A recurring dilemma: how to protect public safety without trampling freedoms. Absolute monarchies, colonial administrations, and even democratic governments repeatedly tested this boundary, sometimes leaning toward repression in crises. The question remains timeless: how much power should police hold in a free society?

5.2. Centralization vs. Local Control

Medieval systems favored local watchmen, while modern states often favored national oversight. Each approach carried pros (uniform standards, resource sharing) and cons (bureaucracy, potential detachment from community concerns). The push-pull between local autonomy and central directives persists.

5.3. Social Equity and Representation

Historically, policing too often served established elites, ignoring or repressing marginalized groups. Modern movements for diversity in police ranks and community policing echo centuries of grievances over partial or prejudiced enforcement. History shows that trust in law enforcement demands some measure of inclusivity and fairness.

5.4. Evolving Role of Technology

From the horse to the automobile, from scribbled ledgers to digital databases, policing adapts to each wave of innovation. But technology can also intensify surveillance or militarization, re-igniting ethical debates about the scope of police power.

6. Concluding Thoughts and Future Implications

6.1. A Complex Heritage

The history of policing is neither purely oppressive nor purely protective. It is a nuanced tapestry: altruistic watchmen, brave detectives, moral paternalism, political manipulation, unbridled brutality, and earnest reforms—all coexisting in different places and eras.

6.2. Building Blocks of Modernity

By the dawn of the 20th century, core features of modern policing—uniformed patrols, centralized bureaus, detective units, partial accountability structures—were in place across much of the world. These institutions would soon be tested by mass warfare, radical revolutions, and the communications revolution of the 20th century.

6.3. Historical Resonances

Present-day controversies—over racial profiling, protest policing, surveillance technologies, militarized units—echo patterns visible throughout this history. Recognizing the deep roots of these debates can inform more balanced, historically aware policy decisions. It reveals that policing problems are not new; they are woven into the social fabric, demanding vigilance, reforms, and thoughtful dialogue about the police's role in a just society.

6.4. Paths Ahead

Even though our account stops at the edge of truly modern times, we can foresee how:

- **Progressive-Era Reforms** in the U.S. or social democratic influences in Europe might continue shaping policing.
- **Colonized Nations** might eventually demand self-determination, reshaping or overthrowing colonial policing structures.
- **Scientific Advances** (fingerprinting perfected, ballistic identification, nascent forensic chemistry) would refine investigative accuracy.
- **International Crises**—world wars, the League of Nations, later the United Nations—would redefine sovereignty and prompt formal policing collaboration.

Hence, the final turn of the 19th to the 20th century stands as a milestone: policing had become a globally recognized institution, indispensable yet perennially contested.

Epilogue: Why This History Matters

Understanding the arc of early and pre-modern policing underscores that law enforcement's evolution was never linear or uncontested. Each culture, epoch, and power structure shaped how police emerged—reflecting and reinforcing social norms, economic arrangements, and political imperatives. Indeed, the "modern police" we know today is less a singular product than a mosaic of legacies: the ancient watch, the medieval reeve, the absolute monarch's guard, the Enlightenment's rational enforcer, the Victorian moral guardian, the colonizer's paramilitary unit, and the detective's scientific approach.

This heritage explains both the remarkable adaptability of policing—spreading to every inhabited region and governance model—and the abiding controversies around its function and fairness. By spotlighting the chapters of the past, we see that calls for reform, accountability, and a balanced approach to civil liberties stretch back centuries. The unresolved tensions persist, inviting current and future generations to learn from historical precedents, to appreciate policing's crucial role in society, but also to guard against its potential excesses.

In closing, this book has traced how policing became a recognized facet of human civilization—encompassing everything from local watchmen to elaborate bureaucracies. While the institution has taken many forms, certain themes recur: the pursuit of order, the challenge of impartiality, the dance between power and the people. This story, though concluding at the threshold of the 20th century, has laid out the core ideas and struggles that continue to shape policing in our contemporary world.

Help Us Share Your Thoughts!

Dear reader,

Thank you for spending your time with this book. We hope it brought you enjoyment and a few new ideas to think about. If there was anything that didn't work for you, or if you have suggestions on how we can improve, please let us know at **kontakt@skriuwer.com**. Your feedback means a lot to us and helps us make our books even better.

If you enjoyed this book, we would be very grateful if you left a review on the site where you purchased it. Your review not only helps other readers find our books, but also encourages us to keep creating more stories and materials that you'll love.

By choosing Skriuwer, you're also supporting **Frisian**—a minority language mainly spoken in the northern Netherlands. Although **Frisian** has a rich history, the number of speakers is shrinking, and it's at risk of dying out. Your purchase helps fund resources to preserve and promote this language, such as educational programs and learning tools. If you'd like to learn more about Frisian or even start learning it yourself, please visit **www.learnfrisian.com**.

Thank you for being part of our community. We look forward to sharing more books with you in the future.

Warm regards,
The Skriuwer Team

www.ingramcontent.com/pod-product-compliance
Lightning Source LLC
LaVergne TN
LVHW012044070526
838202LV00056B/5586